THE FAMILY ALBUM

A Visual History of the New England Historic Genealogical Society, 1845–2020

THE FAMILY ALBUM

A Visual History of the New England Historic Genealogical Society, 1845–2020

Edited by Cécile B. Engeln

Introduction by D. Brenton Simons

NEW ENGLAND HISTORIC
GENEALOGICAL SOCIETY
AmericanAncestors.org

ISBN-13: 978-0-88082-400-2
Library of Congress Control Number: 2020932876

NEW ENGLAND HISTORIC
GENEALOGICAL SOCIETY
AmericanAncestors.org

Boston, Massachusetts
2020

Table of Contents

Acknowledgments vii

Introduction ix

2000 to 2020 x

2020: A Year of Commemoration • Expanding Our Reach • Mayflower 2020 • Family History Benefit Dinners
Wyner Family Jewish Heritage Center • AmericanAncestors.org • Heritage Tours • American Inspiration
The Carolyn A. Lynch Garden • Robert Charles Anderson and the Great Migration Study Project
Scholarship and Publications • Newbury Street Press • Free Fun Friday and Open Newbury
Finding Your Roots • A Special Gathering • Gary Boyd Roberts • Research Services
Scenes from 99–101 Newbury Street • Vita Brevis • American Ancestors Magazine • The Register
Mayflower Descendant

1950 to 2000 32

Sesquicentennial 1995 • Scenes from 99–101 Newbury Street • Scenes from 9 Ashburton Place • In the News

1900 to 1950 46

From the Archives • Scenes from 9 Ashburton Place • Scenes from 18 Somerset Street

1845 to 1900 56

Four Homes • Firsts • Family Treasures • Our Founding

Board and Council 64

Staff 66

Photo Credits 71

Acknowledgments

Many staff members of New England Historic Genealogical Society have contributed to this special commemorative book. D. Brenton Simons was instrumental in getting the project off the ground—coming up with the organization, selecting the photos, and making time to review the text as it evolved. Timothy G. X. Salls and Sally Benny scoured the archives for some of the oldest images, while Claire Vail and Amy Joyce searched for others and digitized them all. The page layout was done by Ellen Maxwell, and all text was researched by Cécile Engeln, who relied on the institutional knowledge of D. Brenton Simons, Timothy G. X. Salls, David Allen Lambert, Christopher Child, Lynn Betlock, Henry B. Hoff, David Dearborn, and Gary Boyd Roberts. It is our sincere hope that you will enjoy this look back at the history and accomplishments of our organization in the last 175 years.

—Sharon Buzzell Inglis
Publishing Director

Introduction

As the nation's founding genealogical institution and largest nonprofit organization of its kind, New England Historic Genealogical Society occupies a central and highly esteemed place in the fields of genealogy and history. In its earliest days, our organization was instrumental in establishing a new scholarly discipline that has had a widespread and lasting impact on the story of America and her peoples. This example has influenced other organizations and sparked similar scholarly efforts around the globe. Today, our mission remains directly about people and heritage: we offer a compelling call for inspirational journeys of personal discovery through genealogy. This work, now embraced by vast worldwide audiences, has, 175 years on, taken much greater root both in popular culture and in academia than our founders could have envisioned in 1845.

Over a long history, we have brought priceless experiences of connection and meaning to generations of Americans. In so doing, New England Historic Genealogical Society and our members have documented the histories of countless individuals and communities—many of which would otherwise never have been gathered, published, or preserved. Now, on the occasion of our 175th anniversary, we are among just a handful of American history organizations thriving at its present great age. Our legacy of service to the public and our present good health can be attributed, in part, to the fact that our organization has always been an innovator—imbued with an entrepreneurial and pioneering spirit. We do not rest on our laurels but, instead, adapt to new constituencies, new technologies, and new approaches, even while championing our traditional core values and upholding the highest standards of genealogical and historical excellence.

Today, New England Historic Genealogical Society flourishes through its broader and more inclusive American Ancestors brand—positively informing an audience of millions of diverse users with more than a billion online records, unprecedented scholarly output and educational initiatives, and the dedicated work of a large cadre of renowned experts and loyal supporters who advance our mission in innumerable ways.

The vibrancy of our beloved organization is captured for all to see in *The Family Album: A Visual History of the New England Historic Genealogical Society, 1845–2020*, along with dozens of historical images, many of which have never been published before. In these pages, you will find a rich—and at times surprising—array of images of our organization's buildings of the past, present, and future; the significant achievements of our scholars, key stakeholders, and members are celebrated herein along with the joy and intellectual vigor of our special events, publications, collections, and much more—all brilliantly illustrated to show the sweep of our progress from a small Victorian reading room to that of a full-bodied cultural icon of international importance. I hope that this visual history, taken in combination with earlier histories of the organization, will share special new insights into almost two centuries of growth, and will, in consonance with our mission to educate, inform, and inspire, serve to engage present and future members in gainful pursuit of the groundbreaking work we do together.

—D. Brenton Simons
President and CEO

2020: A Year of Commemoration

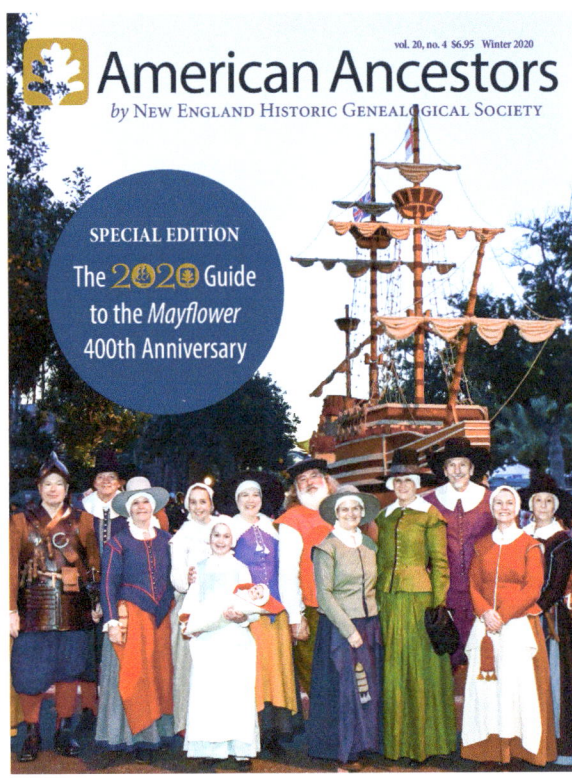

This special issue of *American Ancestors* is devoted entirely to *Mayflower*-themed subjects, including the many 2020 anniversary commemorations. It explores a range of tours, events, resources, and organizations from the United States, Wampanoag Nation, United Kingdom, and the Netherlands.

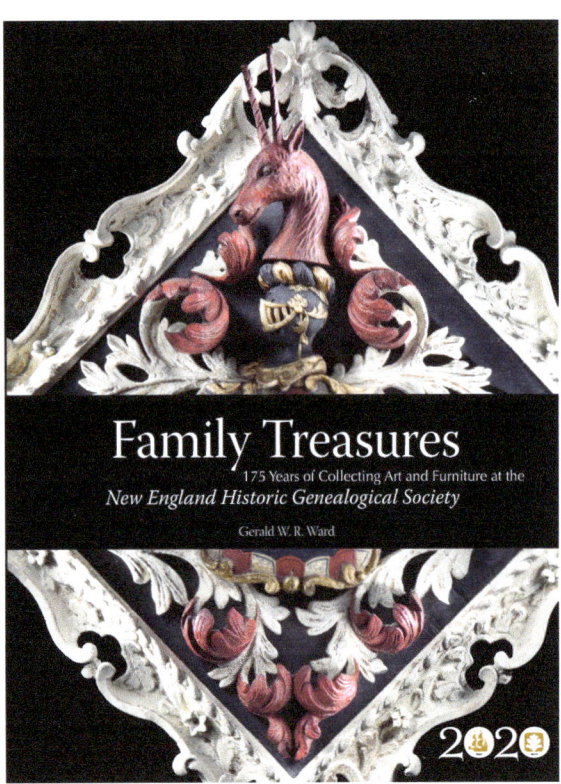

The NEHGS Fine Art Collection is elegantly photographed and displayed throughout the pages of this book, telling the history of the United States through objects and art.

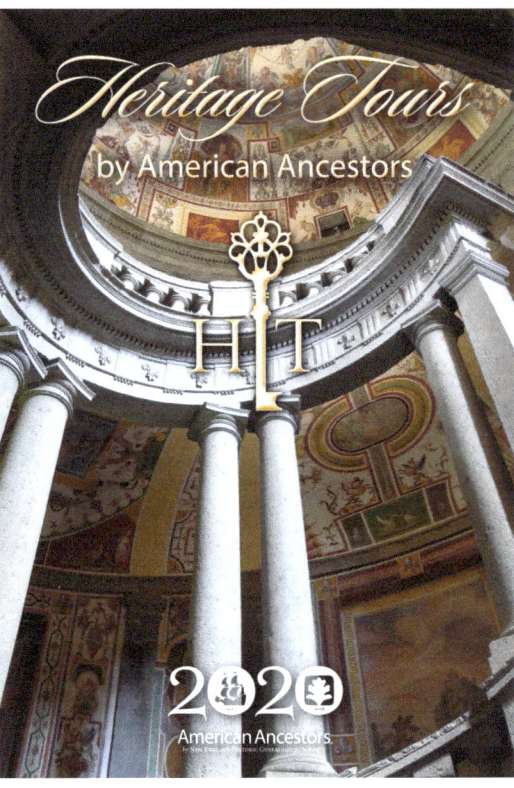

The Heritage Tours brochure for 2020, with tours in Italy, England, Massachusetts, and Virginia.

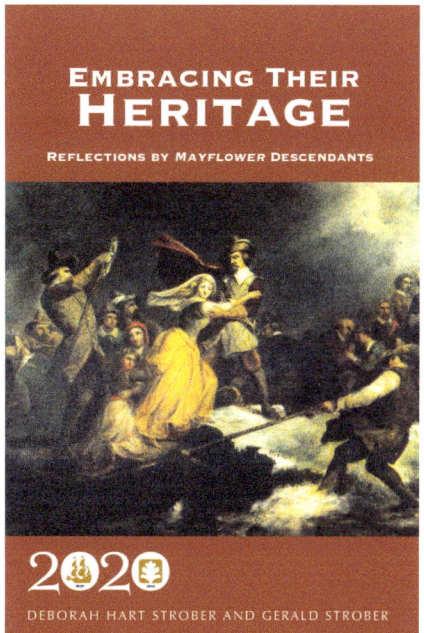

The authors interviewed a wide cross-section of *Mayflower* descendants to recount their varied experiences in discovering their lineage and its impact on their lives.

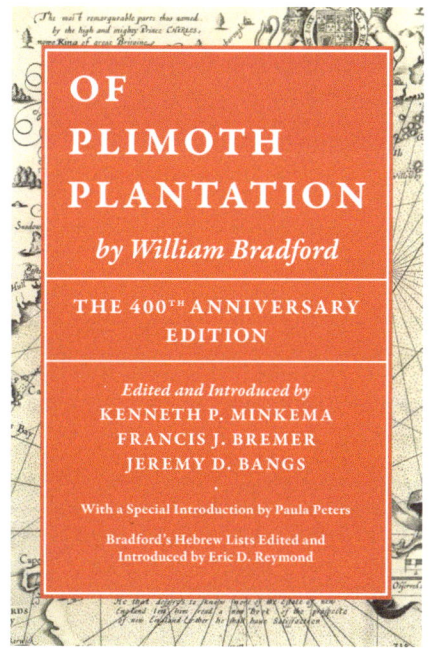

This anniversary edition of William Bradford's magnum opus, made from a new transcription of the original manuscript, includes an introduction that brings together Native and non-Native commentators as well as an appendix that presents Bradford's later Hebrew exercises.

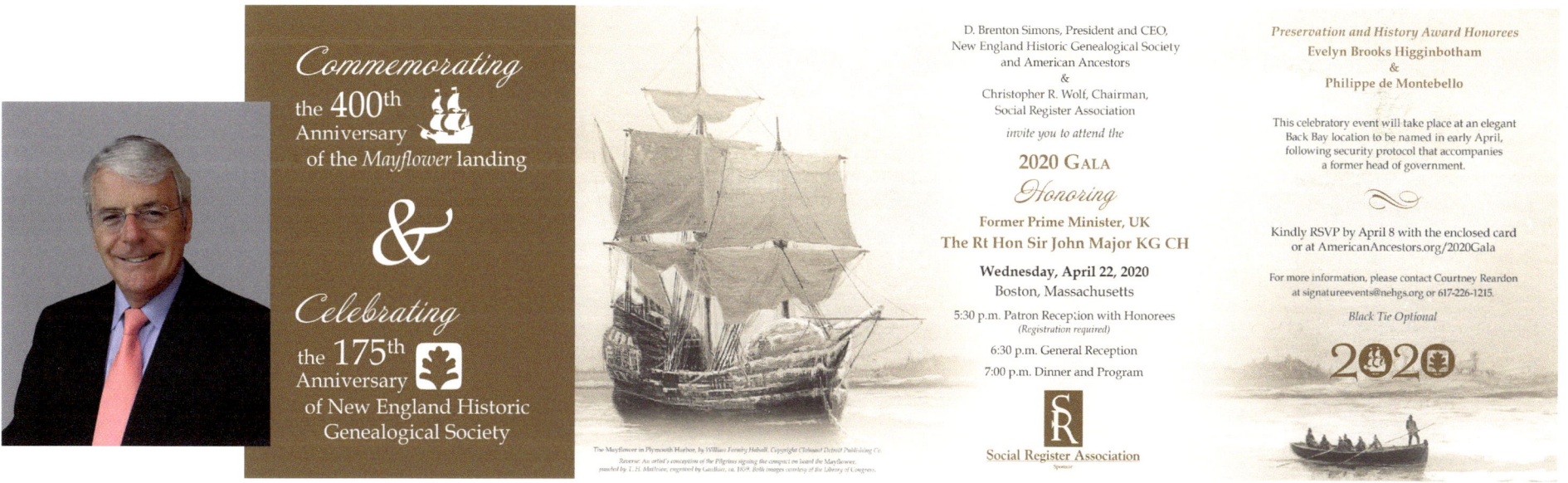

Invitation to New England Historic Genealogical Society's 2020 Gala with former UK Prime Minister Sir John Major.

Expanding Our Reach

Our headquarters expansion—the Cornerstone Project—is a momentous occasion in the history of New England Historic Genealogical Society as we embark to create a national visitor destination on Newbury Street. It will enhance the range of personalized family history services that we offer so we can better serve members across the country as well as reach out to a broader audience and local visitors.

New England Historic Genealogical Society staff members on an outing to the Crane Estate at Castle Hill in Ipswich, Massachusetts, August 27, 2019. As of 2020, our staff numbers 105 professionals.

First row, from left: Emma Brightbill, Kaitlin Hurley, Kyle Lindsay, Cécile Engeln, Ryan Woods, D. Brenton Simons, Trenton Carls, Kyle Hurst, Molly Rogers, and Alice Kane.

Second row: Tim Salls, Don LeClair, Andrew Hanson-Dvoracek, Lindsay Murphy, Valerie Beaudrault, James Heffernan, Susan Fugliese, Rhonda McClure, and Melanie McComb.

Third row: Megan Peterson, Rachel King, Tricia Labbe, Sharon Inglis, Hallie Borstel, Cheryl Gilmore-Thys, and Judy Lucey.

Fourth row: Don Reagan, Alison Kaminsky, Curt DiCamillo, Christopher Child, Ginevra Morse, Ellen Maxwell, Stacie Madden, Rachel Adams, Olga Tugarina, Tom Dreyer, and Geneva Cann.

Mayflower 2020

On April 17, 2019, we held the first of a series of events in the United States commemorating the 400th anniversary of the landing of the *Mayflower*. More than 500 dignitaries, honored guests, members of the press, and the general public gathered for this official Boston launch. Four exhibits that explore 400 years of *Mayflower* and Wampanoag history were unveiled: a scale replica of the *Mayflower*, a sculpture of a Patuxet mother and child recording their family history in wampum, an exhibit on the origins and legacy of the *Mayflower*, and an interactive display on the history of wampum belts.

Harriet Cross, Her Majesty's Consul General to New England, addresses invited guests and the press. Christopher Child, Senior Genealogist and Editor of *Mayflower Descendant*, is dressed as his Pilgrim ancestor John Billington, center.

New England Historic Genealogical Society Chairman Nancy S. Maulsby christens the *Boston Mayflower*, a 1:12 scale model created by artisan Terry Geaghan. Michele Pecoraro, Executive Director of Plymouth 400, at left.

Wampanoag member and President of SmokeSygnals Paula Peters cuts the ribbon of a sculpture of a Patuxet mother and child.

Governor Charlie Baker of Massachusetts appointed D. Brenton Simons to the Plymouth 400th Anniversary Commission. Simons was sworn in as a Commissioner on August 5, 2019, and took the oath administered by Governor Baker on October 30, 2019.

(above and top left) Members of the Wampanoag Nation Singers and Dancers perform at New England Historic Genealogical Society, April 17, 2019.

Family History Benefit Dinners

New England Historic Genealogical Society gathers twice annually for a lively evening in celebration of family history and American heritage. We present our prestigious Lifetime Achievement Award and a detailed family history written by our expert genealogists to a deserving honoree in front of a sparkling array of guests and benefactors.

Honoree and historian Douglas Brinkley with NEHGS Trustee Thomas Bailey Hagen, July 2019.

NEHGS Trustee Bill Griffeth with honoree and broadcast journalist Dan Rather, April 2019.

Honoree and best-selling author David McCullough with NEHGS Executive Vice President and Chief Operating Officer Ryan Woods, April 2018.

Honoree and Pulitzer Prize–winning author Stacy Schiff
with Ryan Woods, April 2017.

Genealogist Eileen Pironti, Publishing Director Sharon Inglis, and
Assistant Publishing Director Cécile Engeln with honoree and author
Winston Groom, October 2017.

D. Brenton Simons with honoree and noted performer
Dame Angela Lansbury, November 2015.

Honoree, former Massachusetts Governor, and 1988 presidential nominee
Michael Dukakis; honoree Kitty Dukakis; and D. Brenton Simons, April 2012.

Martin Hale, Councilor Deborah Campbell Hale, and honoree and filmmaker Ken Burns, April 2011.

Honoree and best-selling author Doris Kearns Goodwin with Trustee Judy Avery, April 2014.

Councilor Joan Bennett Kennedy with honoree and author HRH Princess Michael of Kent, April 2015.

Wyner Family Jewish Heritage Center

In November 2017, New England Historic Genealogical Society became the custodian in perpetuity of the American Jewish Historical Society–New England Archive, and created the Jewish Heritage Center at NEHGS, with the archive as its center. In 2018, it was named the Wyner Family Jewish Heritage Center at NEHGS, in recognition of a cornerstone gift and the long-standing commitment of Justin "Jerry" and Genevieve Wyner.

Wyner Family Jewish Heritage Center Director Rachel King and Jerry Wyner, October 18, 2018.

(*top*) Lindsay Murphy, Rachel King, and Kelsey Sawyer of the JHC. (*middle*) Genevieve Wyner; Bernard Michael, President of the American Jewish Historical Society; Haina Just-Michael; and Jerry Wyner, October 18, 2018. (*bottom*) Launch of the Jewish Heritage Center, November 16, 2017.

AmericanAncestors.org

AmericanAncestors.org is the award-winning website of New England Historic Genealogical Society and home to 1.4 billion searchable names, our online library catalog, digital manuscript collections, educational resources, and online periodicals.

In anticipation of the 2020 commemoration of the *Mayflower* landing, New England Historic Genealogical Society launched the Mayflower 2020 website in November 2017. This interactive website provides extensive resources for researching *Mayflower* passengers, connecting with *Mayflower* descendants, and learning the latest Mayflower 2020 news. The site also features the world's first online gallery of Pilgrim descendants—documenting the ever-increasing diaspora of an estimated 35 million living descendants of the original *Mayflower* passengers around the world. In addtion, we announced a major collaboration with the General Society of Mayflower Descendants and FamilySearch to digitize Mayflower Society applications. Mayflower 2020 was featured on the BBC and NPR, and in the *Boston Globe* and the *Los Angeles Times*.

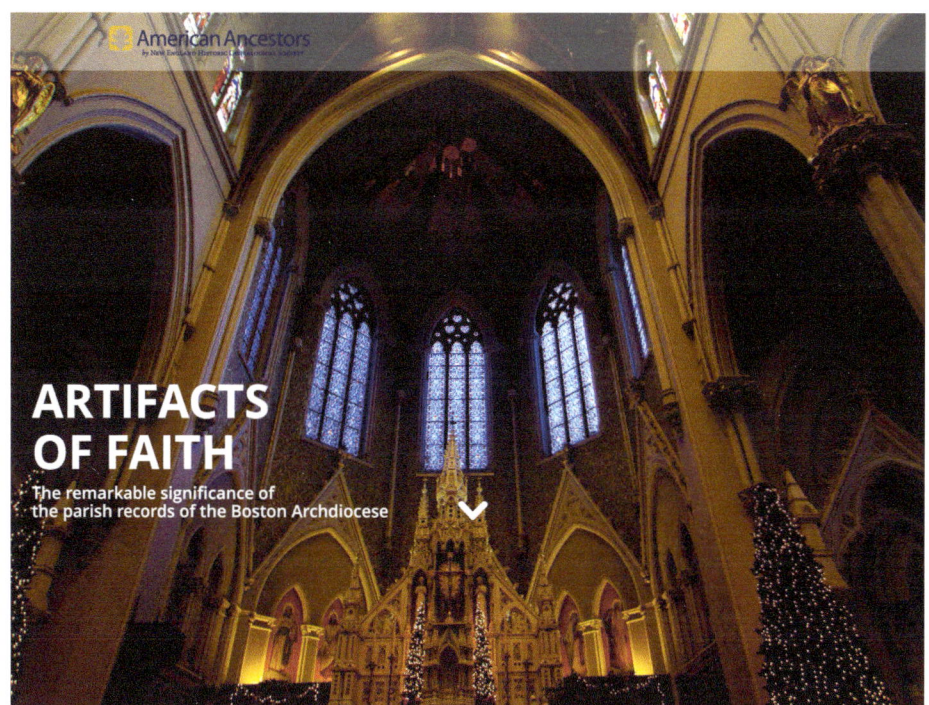

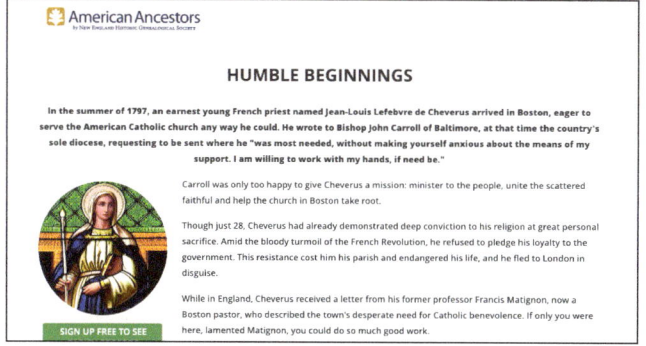

The Historic Catholic Records Online Project, a collaboration between New England Historic Genealogical Society and the Roman Catholic Archdiocese of Boston, was launched in January 2017 on AmericanAncestors.org. It is an online searchable database of millions of sacramental records from over 100 parishes across greater Boston. This is the first time a significant number of sacramental records from any U.S.-based archdiocese has been available in an online digital format.

In June 2019, through a partnership with the Georgetown Memory Project, New England Historic Genealogical Society launched an online research portal at AmericanAncestors.org containing information about the approximately 272 enslaved people who were sold in 1838 by the Georgetown University's Jesuit administrators. The GU272 Memory Project is a unique resource for African American family history and presents the first compiled online data for the GU272 and their descendants.

Heritage Tours

Whether commemorating the 400th anniversary of the landing of the *Mayflower;* exploring the artistic wonders of the United Kingdom, Italy, and beyond; or visiting local treasures closer to home, Heritage Tours offer an opportunity to combine stimulating travel with lifelong learning.

Led by esteemed experts, including Curator Curt DiCamillo and Great Migration author Robert Charles Anderson, our customized itineraries allow for both guided study and independent discovery.

"Palladian Pathways" tour in Italy's Venuto, May 2018. Tour Leader Curt DiCamillo in discussion with Count Valmarana, owner of Villa Rotonda.

"Pilgrim Roots of the Great Migration" tour at Scrooby Manor, Nottingham, England, led by Great Migration expert Robert Charles Anderson, August 2018. Author and official historian of Scrooby Manor Sue Allan is front and center, with hands clasped.

American Inspiration

In September 2019 we launched American Inspiration, our thought-provoking speaker series that presents best-selling authors and their latest books exploring themes of personal identity, families and immigration, and social and cultural history. Curated by Margaret Talcott, Director of Signature and Literary Events, and organized by Courtney Reardon, Events Coordinator, this series is engaging literary audiences in lively dialogues with celebrated writers in our Treat Rotunda.

Our goal is to get educated, inspired, and connect with one another on interesting and important topics while promoting authors and their latest works.

New York Times columnist Gail Collins with Margaret Talcott, October 18, 2019.

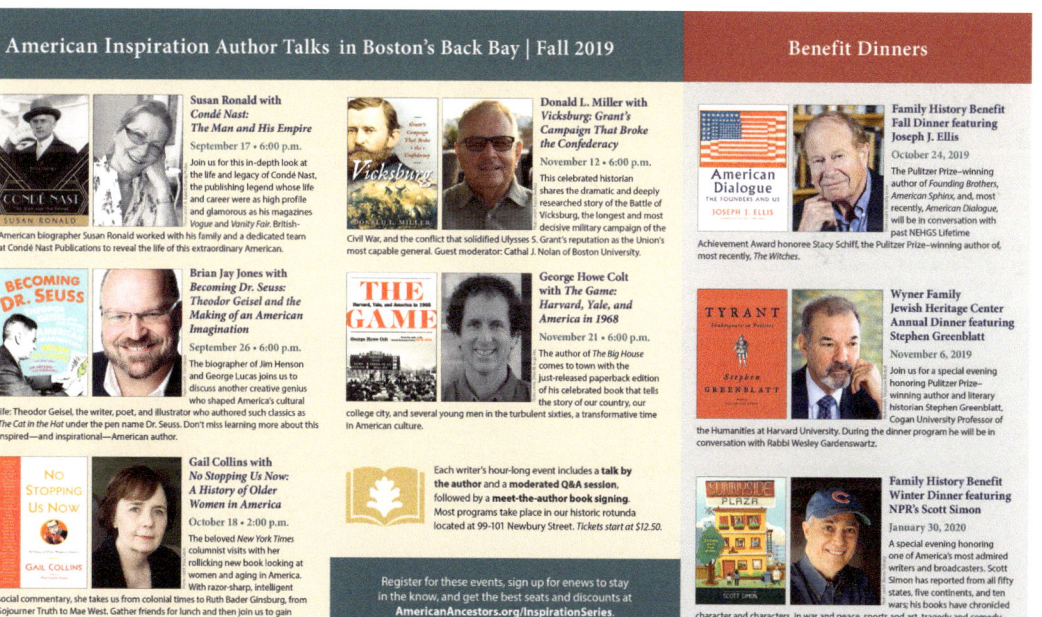

American Inspiration Author Talks in Boston's Back Bay | Fall 2019

Susan Ronald with *Condé Nast: The Man and His Empire*
September 17 • 6:00 p.m.
Join us for this in-depth look at the life and legacy of Condé Nast, the publishing legend whose life and career were as high profile and glamorous as his magazines *Vogue* and *Vanity Fair*. British-American biographer Susan Ronald worked with his family and a dedicated team at Condé Nast Publications to reveal the life of this extraordinary American.

Brian Jay Jones with *Becoming Dr. Seuss: Theodor Geisel and the Making of an American Imagination*
September 26 • 6:00 p.m.
The biographer of Jim Henson and George Lucas joins us to discuss another creative genius who shaped America's cultural life: Theodor Geisel, the writer, poet, and illustrator who authored such classics as *The Cat in the Hat* under the pen name Dr. Seuss. Don't miss learning more about this inspired—and inspirational—American author.

Gail Collins with *No Stopping Us Now: A History of Older Women in America*
October 18 • 2:00 p.m.
The beloved *New York Times* columnist visits with her rollicking new book looking at women and aging in America. With razor-sharp, intelligent social commentary, she takes us from colonial times to Ruth Bader Ginsburg, from Sojourner Truth to Mae West. Gather friends for lunch and then join us to gain insight from Gail Collins, the first woman to hold the post of *New York Times* editorial page editor.

Donald L. Miller with *Vicksburg: Grant's Campaign That Broke the Confederacy*
November 12 • 6:00 p.m.
This celebrated historian shares the dramatic and deeply researched story of the Battle of Vicksburg, the longest and most decisive military campaign of the Civil War, and the conflict that solidified Ulysses S. Grant's reputation as the Union's most capable general. Guest moderator: Cathal J. Nolan of Boston University.

George Howe Colt with *The Game: Harvard, Yale, and America in 1968*
November 21 • 6:00 p.m.
The author of *The Big House* comes to town with the just-released paperback edition of his celebrated book that tells the story of our country, our college city, and several young men in the turbulent sixties, a transformative time in American culture.

Each writer's hour-long event includes a **talk by the author** and a **moderated Q&A session**, followed by a **meet-the-author book signing**. Most programs take place in our historic rotunda located at 99-101 Newbury Street. *Tickets start at $12.50.*

Register for these events, sign up for enews to stay in the know, and get the best seats and discounts at **AmericanAncestors.org/InspirationSeries**.

Further questions? Email signatureevents@nehgs.org or call 617-226-1215 or 888-296-3447.

Benefit Dinners

Family History Benefit Fall Dinner featuring Joseph J. Ellis
October 24, 2019
The Pulitzer Prize–winning author of *Founding Brothers*, *American Sphinx*, and, most recently, *American Dialogue*, will be in conversation with past NEHGS Lifetime Achievement Award honoree Stacy Schiff, the Pulitzer Prize–winning author of, most recently, *The Witches*.

Wyner Family Jewish Heritage Center Annual Dinner featuring Stephen Greenblatt
November 6, 2019
Join us for a special evening honoring Pulitzer Prize–winning author and literary historian Stephen Greenblatt, Cogan University Professor of the Humanities at Harvard University. During the dinner program he will be in conversation with Rabbi Wesley Gardenswartz.

Family History Benefit Winter Dinner featuring NPR's Scott Simon
January 30, 2020
A special evening honoring one of America's most admired writers and broadcasters. Scott Simon has reported from all fifty states, five continents, and ten wars; his books have chronicled character and characters, in war and peace, sports and art, tragedy and comedy.

Flyer displaying American Inspiration's inaugural season.

The Carolyn A. Lynch Garden

In 2011, under the leadership of Vice Chairman of the Board of Trustees Carolyn A. Lynch and with the support of generous donors, New England Historic Genealogical Society undertook the important task of beautifying and improving access to our building through the creation of a new garden and entryway.

On October 1, 2015, Carolyn A. Lynch died in Marblehead, Massachusetts, aged 69. She was a longtime trustee of NEHGS and served on several committees, helping to guide and shape our organization at a pivotal time in our history.

Garden Committee member Kelly McCoulf, Chairman Eric B. Schultz, Boston Mayor Thomas M. Menino, Garden Committee Chair and Vice Chairman Carolyn Lynch, President and CEO D. Brenton Simons, and Garden Committee members David Bruce and Ginger Koster take part in the ribbon cutting, 2011.

On June 8, 2018, New England Historic Genealogical Society honored Carolyn A. Lynch in a ceremony dedicating the courtyard garden in her memory. Members of the Lynch family and the Lynch Foundation were in attendance. Peter Lynch and D. Brenton Simons spoke of her dedication to NEHGS and her love of gardening; Cardinal Seán O'Malley blessed the garden in her memory.

Peter Lynch and Cardinal O'Malley with Peter and Carolyn's daughters: Annie Lukowski, Elizabeth de Montrichard, and Mary Witkowski, 2018.

New England Historic Genealogical Society staff members on an outing to the Peabody Essex Museum in Salem, Massachusetts, June 5, 2018.

First row, from left: Alice Kane, Susan Donnelly, Christopher Child, Christopher Russell, Kelsey Sawyer, Jessie Xu, Cécile Engeln, Ellen Maxwell, Ryan Woods, D. Brenton Simons, Beth Brown, Michelle Norris, Nancy Bernard, Emily Baldoni, Megan Peterson, Emma Brightbill, Henry Hornblower, Olga Tugarina, Tom Dreyer, Meaghan Siekman, and David Allen Lambert.

Second row: Steven Solomon, Sharon Inglis, Lindsay Murphy, Helen Herzer, Lena Sparks, Tim Salls, Jenna LaRiviere, Kyle Lindsay, James Heffernan, Jeremy Bento, Lynn Betlock, Curt DiCamillo, Sarah Dery, Jason Amos, Mary Freed, Andrew Hanson-Dvoracek, Lindsay Fulton, Ginevra Morse, Sheilagh Doerfler, Don LeClair, Tricia Labbe, Michael Forbes, Sally Benny, Rachel Adams, Eileen Pironti, Kathleen Kaldis, Jeanne Belmonte, and Molly Rogers.

Robert Charles Anderson and the Great Migration Study Project

Between 1620 and 1640 about 20,000 men, women, and children crossed the Atlantic to settle New England. The Great Migration Study Project, founded by Robert Charles Anderson, FASG, provides a concise, reliable summary of research on these early immigrants to America. This effort began in 1988 and has resulted in more than 2,400 in-depth sketches on New England's earliest settlers and the discovery of many previously unidentified immigrants. In a series published by New England Historic Genealogical Society, Anderson has provided accounts on most of them. His works have led thousands of family historians to discover ancestral connections to these earliest settlers in our country's history.

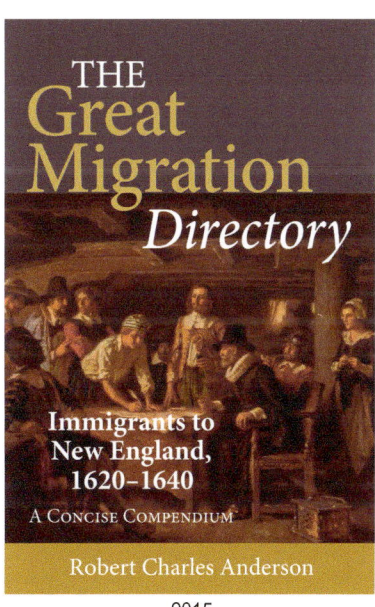

2015

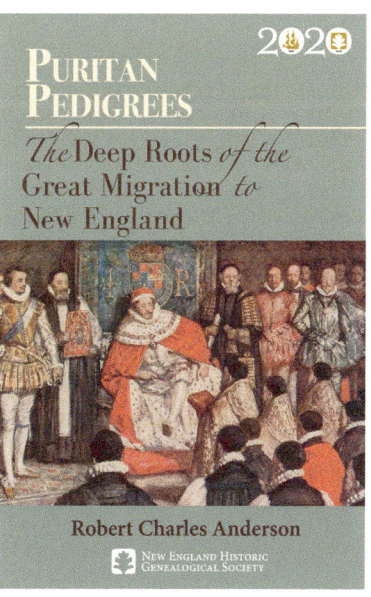

2018

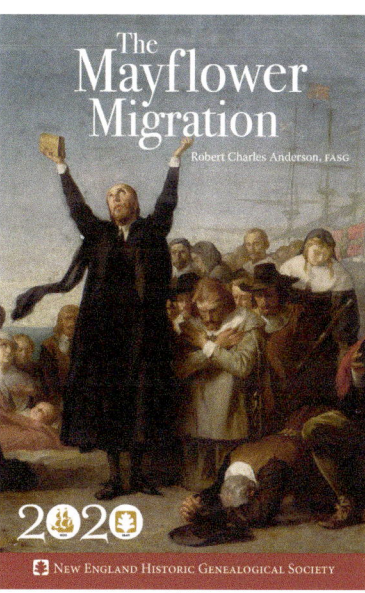

2020

Scholarship and Publications

For almost two hundred years we have published the most important sources in family history—articles, source records, compiled genealogies, scholarly compendia, methodological guides, and much more. Today, with Publishing Director Sharon Inglis and the dedicated Publications team, we publish twenty books or more a year.

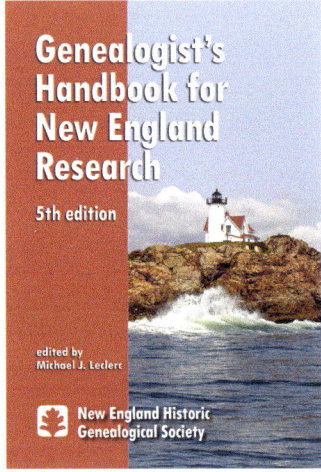

2012

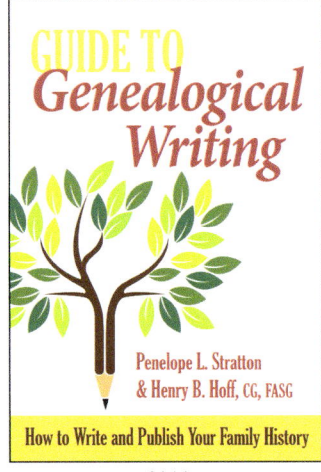

2014

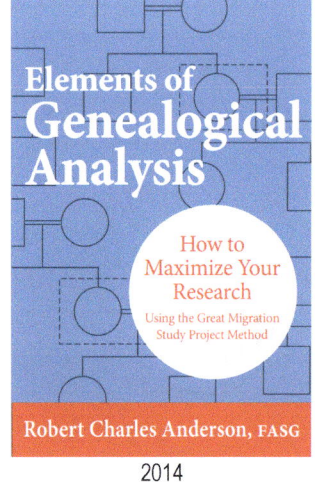

2014

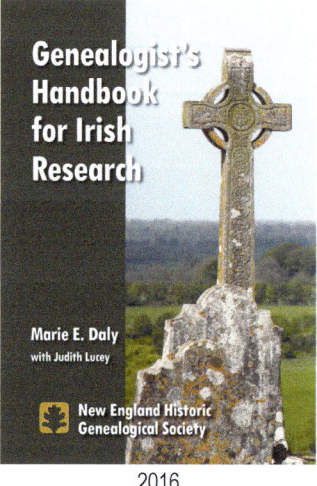

2016

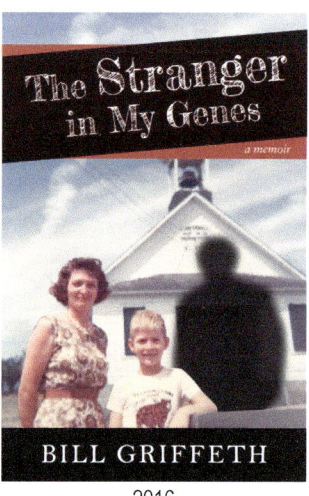

2016

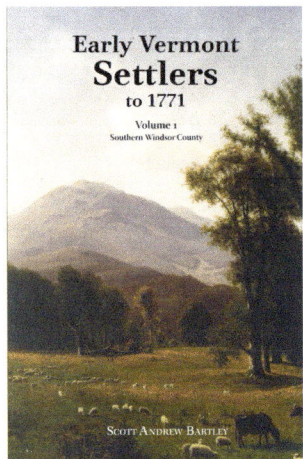

2017

2018

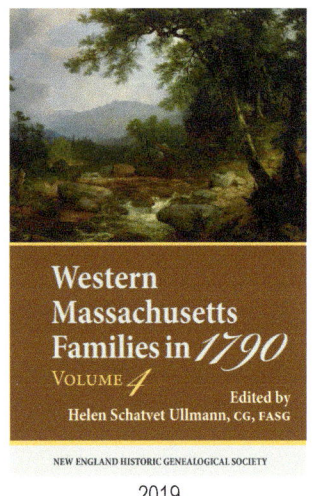

2019

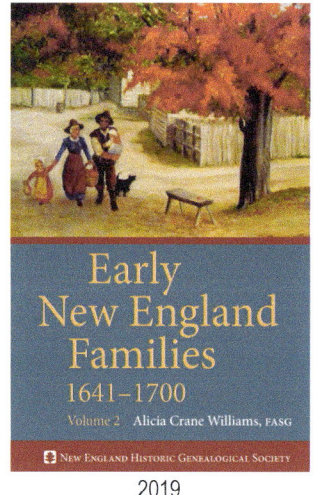

2019

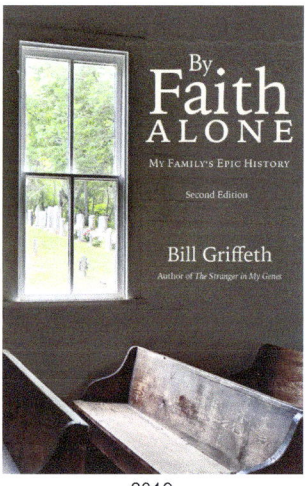

2019

Newbury Street Press

Newbury Street Press, established at New England Historic Genealogical Society in 1996, is the premier publisher of family histories in America. The expert genealogists of the Newbury Street Press build on our history of publishing compiled genealogies of enduring value. These books represent our high standards of documentation and authentication of genealogical research.

Published in 2018; winner of the National Genealogical Society Award for Excellence in Writing: Genealogy and Family History.

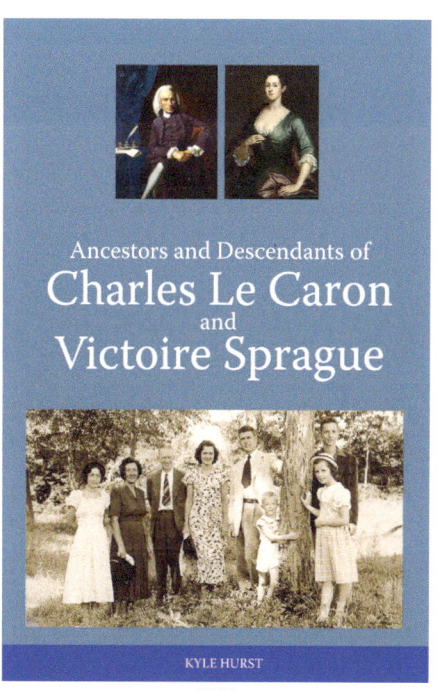

2020

2019

2017

2011

Free Fun Friday and Open Newbury

Sponsored by the Highland Street Foundation, Free Fun Fridays enable Massachusetts cultural venues to offer free admission to the general public. New England Historic Genealogical Society has been participating since 2011, offering genealogy-related projects for kids, introductory lectures by our expert genealogists, research assistance, database access, library tours, and membership discounts.

Since 2017, New England Historic Genealogical Society has been an active participant in the city of Boston's Open Newbury program. Held on three Sundays in July, August, and September, the busy thoroughfare of Newbury Street is closed to vehicular traffic and transformed into a festive promenade featuring local musicians, food trucks, sidewalk sales, and more. Attracting students, families, tourists, and Bostonians alike, each event brings thousands of visitors to our tent outside 99–101 Newbury Street and affords us an incredible opportunity to engage new audiences and inspire the next generation of family historians.

(*above, left*) A young visitor places a pin on a world map representing her ancestor's origins during Open Newbury.

(*above*) NEHGS Education Coordinator Tricia Labbe and Senior Researcher James Heffernan in costume at Free Fun Friday, July 7, 2017.

(*left*) Chief Genealogist David Allen Lambert in consulation with a visitor.

Finding Your Roots

Since 2013, New England Historic Genealogical Society has proudly been the anchor filming location for the PBS TV series *Finding Your Roots with Henry Louis Gates, Jr.* Additionally, our Research Services department has served as genealogical fact-checkers for the series since 2016.

Finding Your Roots, now in its sixth season, is the brainchild of NEHGS Trustee and Harvard University professor Henry Louis "Skip" Gates, Jr. In 2010, we honored him with our Lifetime Achievement Award. Included with the award was a detailed family history, including a foreword by Oprah Winfrey.

Dr. Henry Louis Gates, Jr., and Jim Powers, Jr., Location Manager for New England Historic Genealogical Society, surrounded by the *Finding Your Roots* crew in the Treat Rotunda.

(*above*) Dr. Henry Louis Gates, Jr., and crew in the Reading Room.
(*top right*) Dr. Henry Louis Gates, Jr., with D. Brenton Simons in the Treat Rotunda.

New England Historic Genealogical Society staff members in front of *Mayflower II* on an outing to Plimoth Plantation, Plymouth, Massachusetts, October 9, 2015.

First row, from left: Eva Murphy, Tom Dreyer, Olga Tugarina, Jean Powers, Rhonda McClure, Emily Baldoni, Jennifer Guerin, Kelly McCoulf, Sarah DiMariano, Ryan Woods, D. Brenton Simons, Beth Brown, Dani Torres, Kyle Hurst, Gabby Passaro, Judy Lucey, Deborah Rossi, John Phlo, Henry Hornblower, and Susan Harrington.

Second row: Jason Amos, Jeanne Belmonte, Michael Forbes, Christopher Child, Sam Sturgis, Jim Power, Michelle Major, Lynn Betlock, Timothy G. X. Salls, Steven Shilcusky, Ginevra Morse, Steven Solomon, Rick Park, Tricia Labbe, Sally Benny, Helen Herzer, Kathleen Mackenzie, Sarah Liebenrood, Jeremy Bento, Christopher Carter, and Andrew Krea.

A Special Gathering

On the occasion of his twentieth anniversary at New England Historic Genealogical Society, D. Brenton Simons was honored at a special gathering with past executive directors and chairmen, October 24, 2013.

First row, from left: Eric B. Schultz (Chairman, 2008–2012), David H. Burnham (Chairman, 2012–2017), D. Brenton Simons (President*, 2005 to present), Rodney Armstrong (Chairman, 1977–1982), Ralph J. Crandall (Executive Director, 1982–1987, 1988–2005).

Back row: William M. Fowler Jr. (Chairman, 1991–1996), John W. Sears (Executive Director, 1987), John G. L. Cabot (Chairman, 1996–2002), David W. Kruger (Chairman, 2002–2008).

*The title Executive Director was changed to President and CEO on April 23, 2006.

Gary Boyd Roberts

Gary Boyd Roberts is Senior Research Scholar Emeritus at New England Historic Genealogical Society, with which he has been associated since 1974.

Considered one of the greatest genealogical minds of his generation, Roberts is the author of *American Ancestors and Cousins of The Princess of Wales; Notable Kin*, volumes one and two; *The Best Genealogical Sources in Print*, volume one; *Ancestors of American Presidents, The Royal Descents of 900 Immigrants to the American Colonies, Quebec, or the United States; The Mayflower 500: Five Hundred Notable Descendants of the Founding Fathers of the Mayflower*; and many articles, introductions, and columns.

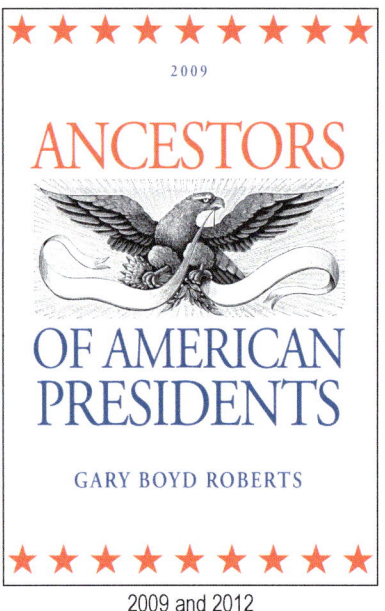

2009 and 2012

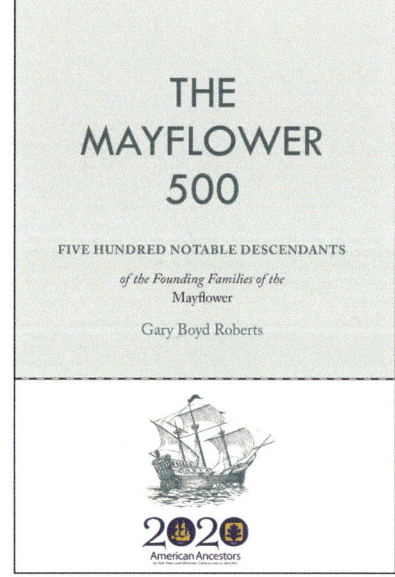

2020

Gary Boyd Roberts's seminar marking the publication of his book, *The Royal Descents of 900 Immigrants to the American Colonies, Quebec, or the United States*, Treat Rotunda, September 29, 2018.

Research Services

Research Services is an enthusiastic and dedicated team led by Director of Research Services Lindsay Fulton. With 1,288 research cases in 2019, they consistently help clients knock down brick walls, apply to lineage societies, and find proof of their families in written records.

Research Services offices, fourth floor.

Members of the Research Services team in the Reading Room. *Front, from left:* Sheilagh Doerfler, Geneva Cann, Raymond Addison, Lindsay Fulton, Elizabeth Peay, Chloe Jones; *back:* Sarah Dery, Hallie Borstel, Katrina Fahy, James Heffernan, Danielle Cournoyer, Jennica Baynes, Michelle Norris.

Scenes from 99–101 Newbury Street

Seventh location of New England Historic Genealogical Society, 1964 to present.

Renovated library, fourth floor, where Microform readers, CDs, and map collections are found.

The Bookstore at NEHGS, first floor.

The Treat Rotunda, first floor, was named in 2000 in honor of NEHGS Patrons William and Vivian Treat.

Alice Kane, Library Patron Services and Consultations Manager, with library patrons in the Reading Room.

The Board Room after its mini-renovation in 2015.

Visitors in the Ruth Chauncy Bishop Reading Room.

Vita Brevis, the blog of New England Historic Genealogical Society, is designed to offer the reader short essays as well as news of the greater genealogical community. It includes posts on research methods—applicable to a variety of genealogical subjects—as well as results. Like a mosaic, these posts have already become a resource for genealogical researchers to explore.

With more than two million page views in the life of the blog (launched in January 2014), *Vita Brevis* has become an important part of its readers' daily routine.

Vita Brevis turns five

🕐 January 10, 2019   📁 Genealogical Writing, News, Technology   🏷 A Genealogist's Diary, Great Migration Study Project, Object Lessons, Photographs, Serendipity, Spotlight   👤 Scott C. Steward

Photos by Claire Vail

When I became Editor-in-Chief at NEHGS in June 2013, one of the new initiatives Ryan Woods and I discussed was a blog for the Society. Current and former colleagues worked with me to establish the blog's purpose and name, and – in time – got me set up on WordPress. (Two years later, when I was on a sabbatical, three current and former colleagues managed the blog in my absence.) So *Vita Brevis* has been a cooperative venture from the beginning, relying on the energy and commitment of the NEHGS staff and some dedicated outside contributors to produce fresh content.

Today marked the fifth anniversary of the blog's official launch, with a post by Robert Charles Anderson. Coincidentally, Bob has a new book out, while tomorrow will mark the blog's 1,250th published post. (In a few days *Vita Brevis* posts will have been read two million times.)

Naturally, we marked all of these things with a cake. (The saga of the cake's creation is an amazing one; kudos to Claire Vail, who had the cake made and took all of these photographs.)

We managed to wrangle a few of the blog's contributors to admire the cake. They are, from left to right, Jean Maguire, Ryan Woods, Ellen Maxwell, Scott Steward, Cécile Engeln, Don LeClair, Chris Child, Bob Anderson, Sharon Inglis, Lynn Betlock, and Brenton Simons.

Generatio longa, vita brevis

🕐 January 2, 2014   📁 Family Stories, News, Research Methods   👤 New England Historic Genealogical Society

Welcome to *Vita Brevis*, the blog of the New England Historic Genealogical Society. *Vita Brevis* is designed to offer the reader short essays by the Society's expert staff on their own research as well as news of the greater genealogical community.

As the nation's oldest genealogical Society, the NEHGS collection has always contained books and manuscripts on other subjects than New England; now, with its growing database collection, NEHGS is truly a national – and an international – resource for family history.

Vita Brevis will include short posts on research methods – applicable to a variety of genealogical subjects – as well as posts on results. Like a mosaic, these posts will, in time, form a new collection for the genealogical researcher to explore.

Editor-in-Chief Scott Steward celebrates the 5-year anniversary of *Vita Brevis*, January 2019.

American Ancestors Magazine

American Ancestors magazine—available in print and as an online publication— covers a wide range of genealogical topics and is led by our magazine team: Lynn Betlock, Carolyn Oakley, and Jean Powers. It appeals to family historians of all levels and includes topics such as useful sources, helpful research strategies, compelling historical accounts, and interesting case studies. First published in 2000 as *New England Ancestors*, the name changed to *American Ancestors: New England, New York, and Beyond* in 2010. Eventually the title was changed again to *American Ancestors* to reflect our growing nationwide expertise.

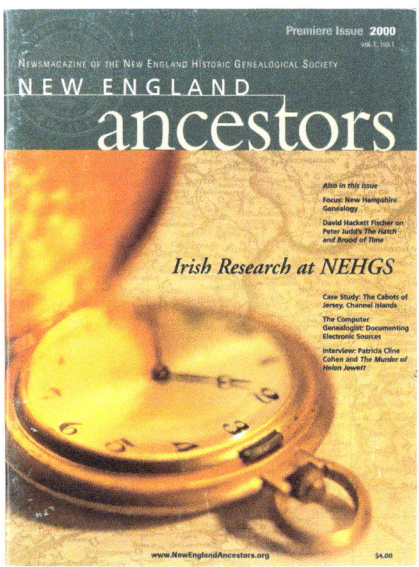

Cover of the first issue of *New England Ancestors*, 2000.

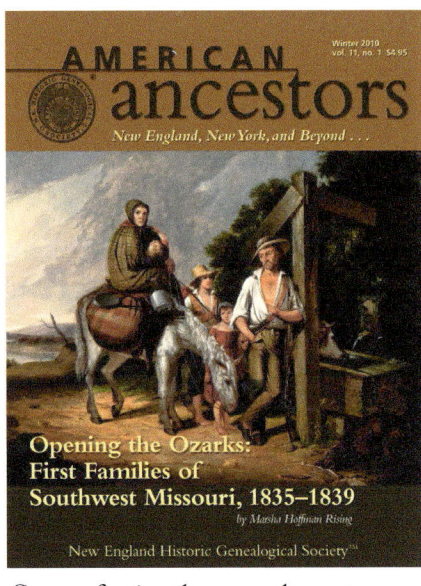

Cover reflecting the name change to *American Ancestors: New England, New York, and Beyond*, 2010.

Recent covers of *American Ancestors*.

The Register

Published quarterly since 1847, the *Register: The Journal of American Genealogy* is the oldest in the field, focusing on authoritative compiled genealogies. The *Register* has been edited by Henry B. Hoff and Helen Schatvet Ullmann since 2001, and was redesigned in 2015. Articles solve genealogical problems, identify immigrant origins, or present treatments of multiple generations.

Mayflower Descendant

First published in 1899 by George Ernest Bowman, founder of the Massachusetts Society of Mayflower Descendants, *Mayflower Descendant* has long been a highly regarded source of scholarship on the subject *Mayflower* families and related genealogies, their origins in England, and their lives and places of residence in America, from the earliest settlements to their migrations north and westward. In 2015, New England Historic Genealogical Society assumed stewardship of the venerable journal and appointed Editor Christopher Child. *Mayflower Descendant* continues to be a significant source of genealogical and historical scholarship.

Sesquicentennial 1995

In July 1995, New England Historic Genealogical Society held the Sesquicentennial Conference to celebrate its 150th anniversary. The four-day conference of lectures, exhibits, presentations, and banquets drew over 1,600 participants. Speakers included author David McCullough and Professor Laurel Thatcher Ulrich.

Author David McCullough, Chairman William M. Fowler Jr., and Reference Librarian Jerome E. Anderson.

Supreme Court Justice David Hackett Souter and longtime Executive Director Ralph J. Crandall.

Board Member and Sesquicentennial Chairman Sandi Hewlett with Executive Director Ralph J. Crandall at podium.

Over 1,600 participants attended the Sesquicentennial Conference at Westin Hotel, Copley Place, Boston, 1995.

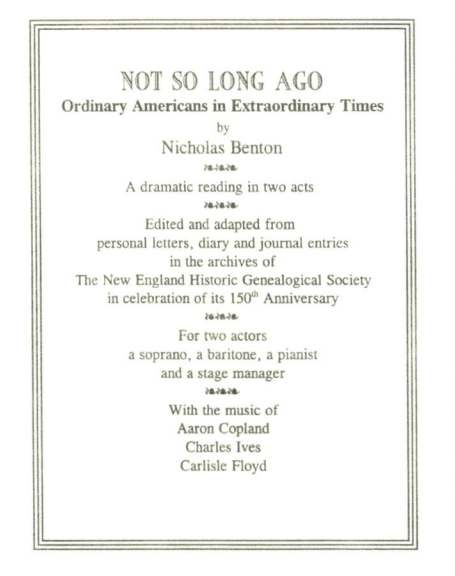

NOT SO LONG AGO
Ordinary Americans in Extraordinary Times
by
Nicholas Benton

A dramatic reading in two acts

Edited and adapted from
personal letters, diary and journal entries
in the archives of
The New England Historic Genealogical Society
in celebration of its 150th Anniversary

For two actors
a soprano, a baritone, a pianist
and a stage manager

With the music of
Aaron Copland
Charles Ives
Carlisle Floyd

Academy-award winning actress Celeste Holm and Tim Clark during rehearsal for *Not So Long Ago*. This play by Nicholas Benton, written from original materials in our collections, was produced by New England Historic Genealogical Society at the Maxwell Theatre in the Museum of Our National Heritage, in Lexington, Massachusetts, on October 21, 1995. It was directed by Benton, Vice President of New England Historic Genealogical Society, 1988–1993.

Title page of the script for *Not So Long Ago* (1995).

New England Historic Genealogical Society staff in August 1994, in the Reading Room.

First row, from left: Jackie Kamlot, W. Denis Hanley, Julie Helen Otto, Marshall K. Kirk, Gary Boyd Roberts, Virginia B. Augerson, Robert Shaw, Shirely L. Bartlett.

Second row: John Phlo, Allison Dyson Johnson, Ann L. Dzindolet, Marie E. Daly, Dennis P. Dahill, Eleanor Yee, Janet Mullen, Susan W. Gillespie, Jane Fletcher Fiske, Lynne Burke, Scott Andrew Bartley, and Barbara J. Robinson.

Third row: David A. Lambert, Mary S. Erlewine, Gomer U. Sanchez, Kenneth S. Paulsen, D. Brenton Simons, Jerome E. Anderson, Nathaniel N. Shipton.

Scenes from 99–101 Newbury Street

Seventh location of New England Historic Genealogical Society, 1964 to present.

Historian John Schutz, longtime Secretary of the NEHGS Board of Trustees and author of *A Noble Pursuit: The Sesquicentennial History of the New England Historic Genealogical Society, 1845–1995*, using the library's microfilm collection, ca. 1990.

Executive Director Ralph J. Crandall and George Redmonds, the noted surname expert from Yorkshire, England, who led our English tours for many years, ca. 1990.

Director of User Access Services Maureen Taylor, ca. 1990. Taylor is a popular author and researcher who is also known as "the Photo Detective."

Reading Room, ca. 1980–1990.

Circulating library, ca. 1980.

New England Historic Genealogical Society staff in 1983, in the old third-floor Trustees Room at 101 Newbury Street.

From front left: Gary Boyd Roberts, Volunteer Steven Burns, David Curtis Dearborn, Alice I. Ledogar, *Register* Assistant Editor Donald M. Nielson, Elizabeth Hersey, Comptroller Dorothy M. Daybre, Director Ralph J. Crandall (center), Christopher P. O'Sullivan, *Register* Editor Edward W. Hanson, Linda Naylor, Nathaniel N. Shipton, James C. Agnew, Danny Williams, and Valentine Bean.

NEHGS volunteer using a Microfiche reader.

Microfiche carousels containing the International Genealogical Index produced by the Family History Library of The Church of Jesus Christ of Latter-day Saints. Today, this is found online.

One of the two Zenith Heathkit Z120 computers used by NEHGS volunteers to prepare the cumulative index to vols. 51–148 of the *Register*, an arduous task. The computers had no hard drive and the floppy disks it accepted held little data. The publication of the *Register* index was a milestone for NEHGS, as it allowed wider access to the contents of the *Register*.

Reference Librarian David Dearborn, center, ca. 1980.

Offices, 1980.

NEHGS volunteers and research staff, ca. 1980–1990s.

New England Historic Genealogical Society staff in December 1974, in the Reading Room.

First row, from left: Director James Brugler Bell, Diane MacLachlan, Comptroller Dorothy M. Daybre, Cynthia D. Fleming, Assistant *Register* Editor Susan L. Patterson, Anne Pulling, and Mary Haskell.

Second row: George DeMetz, Associate *Register* Editor Ralph J. Crandall, Margaret Hazen, Stuart F. Myers, David Hall, Henry P. Blakeslee, Reference Librarian Gary Boyd Roberts, and Burgess E. Nichols.

New England Historic Genealogical Society, ca. 1980.

Architect's design for New England Historic Genealogical Society at 99–101 Newbury Street, 1964.

Rabbi Malcolm Stern, center, in the Treat Rotunda at New England Historic Genealogical Society, April 9, 1979. NEHGS and the American Jewish Historical Society hosted a reception upon the publication of Rabbi Stern's book, *First American Jewish Families: 600 Genealogies, 1654–1977* (1978). The book provides information on every family of Jewish origin known to have been established in the United States prior to 1840, and traces them to the present where possible. Rabbi Stern was the President of the American Society of Genealogists and the authority on Jewish genealogy at the time.

NEXUS

THE BIMONTHLY NEWSLETTER OF
THE NEW ENGLAND HISTORIC GENEALOGICAL SOCIETY

VOL. II, NUMBER 3   JUNE 1985   BOSTON, MASSACHUSETTS

Library Hours, Tuesday-Saturday 9 AM-4:45 PM. Loan Library Hours, Monday-Saturday 9 AM-4:45 PM

Governor Dukakis Proclaims Family History Week in Massachusetts

Governor Michael S. Dukakis recently proclaimed the week of May 12-18 as Family History Week in Massachusetts. He is shown here signing the proclamation. Gathered at the ceremony in his office are, left to right: Joseph Guertin, President of the Berkshire Family History Association; Dr. Ralph Crandall, Director of the New England Historic Genealogical Society; Rose Morrison, President of the Plymouth County Chapter of MASSOG (Mass. Society of Genealogists); Helen Breen of Essex Society of Genealogists; David Robertson, Immediate Past President of MASSOG, and representing Suffolk County; Marie Daiey, President of TIARA (The Irish Ancestral Research Assn.); Shirley Barnes, President of Concord Genealogical Round Table; James Nesbit, President of MASSOG; Ernestine ("June") Rose, President of Essex Society of Genealogists; Sheila Fitzpatrick, President of Middlesex Chapter of MASSOG; and Robert Starratt, President of the Massachusetts Genealogical Council.

NEXUS was first published in 1983. A new member benefit, the magazine was intended to be "... a more informal way for members to communicate with one another through the query column, notices of family reunions, research in progress, interesting articles and other letters and communications," as stated in its preliminary issue. The publication later became *NEXUS: The Newsmagazine of the New England Historic Genealogical Society* and continued through 1999.

Scenes from 9 Ashburton Place

Sixth location of New England Historic Genealogical Society, 1912 to 1964.

Three views of the library, ca. 1960.

Library, 1959.

Librarians Diana Benson Small, Edith Eliza Hazelton, and Mildred Evelyn Leavitt, 1959.

Library stacks, 1960.

IN THE NEWS

Largest Genealogical Society in World in Boston

By ELIZABETH WATTS

"Please send me a list of buried treasures."

"When did the English sparrow come to America?"

"Did Betsy Ross allow cats in the shop where she worked?"

These are questions typical of those that are addressed to historical societies and the New England Historic Genealogical Society is no exception. In fact, since it's the largest society of its kind anywhere in the world, they get rather more than their share.

Look in on Dr. Arthur Adams, eminent genealogist, professor emeritus of Trinity College, and present librarian of the Society, in his book-filled room at 9 Ashburton Place and you'll find his desk heaped high with correspondence.

"Many of these request family data," points out Dr. Adams, "but we get our proportion of unanswerable questions, too."

★ ★ ★

More than 170,000 books are housed in the main library of the Society and two doors down at 7 Ashburton Place there are 20,000 more in the Directory Library.

★ ★ ★

The Society's collection of New England data is the greatest in the world. From manuscripts and from family letters, from books and from records, the family trees of thousands of New Englanders can be traced back to the time of their original settling in this country.

In spite of the pressure of contemporary living, people seem to be just as interested as they ever were in making the leisurely trip back through family histories.

"Attendance stays just the same," says Dr. Adams whose home is on Pinckney st., just the other side of the hill from the society building. "There is an increase in heraldry, though."

"This year the library was used by 3109 persons, a slightly larger number than last year," says Dr. Adams. "Visitors registered from 44 states and from six foreign countries. During the year, 1228 volumes, 1844 pamphlets and 383 miscellaneous items have been added to the library, a total of 2465 items."

Each year finds new material, some of which fills in one square in the patchwork of New England names and family histories being sent to the society.

Among the contributors last year was Herbert N. Hixon of West Medway who gave the society John Boyd's Orderly Book, a rare find

MAIL FROM ALL OVER the country crosses the desk of Dr. Arthur Adams, Librarian for the New England Historic Genealogical Society on Ashburton Place.

which included a list of the West Medway deaths from 1825 to 1920.

★ ★ ★

In 1845 when the Society was founded, no historical society directing its energies solely to genealogical research existed anywhere in the world. Valuable records and family chronicles were being lost and destroyed because there was no general and logical destiny for them.

In the early days of this country, the past, from which the hardy settlers were trying to escape, was representative of tyranny. Landed gentry and hereditary titles spelled the privileges of a world they wanted no part of. So the succeeding New England records became even more important.

Family histories can be traced across the Atlantic, though at the Society. "How about a fourth or

fifth generation Irishman who wanted to find his family's relatives in the old country?" Dr. Adams was asked.

★ ★ ★

"If he knows the town or even the county where his family came from that's a good head start," pointed out Dr. Adams. "Of course many valuable records were burned or destroyed during the Rebellion but even so there's a good chance he could find out what he wants to know."

★ ★ ★

"Fascinating" is the word Mrs. Joseph Curtis Howes of Brookline uses to describe the work she does at the Society as curator. "I've gotten so I don't tell people how long I've worked here," she says with a smile, "but you can discover something new and unusual every day." One of her special interests is the Atkinson-Lancaster collection, willed to the Society by Lizzie Daniel Rose Atkinson, a member in 1933. Housed in a fireproof vault, the handsome collection of Federal and Colonial period treasures includes everything from a silver flower and handkerchief holder to a pair of Russian shoes with split wooden soles brought back by Capt Caleb Cook of Salem from one of his voyages.

★ ★ ★

There are Indian Apache playing cards painted on buffalo skin, a lock of Garibaldi's hair ("who was Delilah, I Wonder," puts in Mrs. Howes), an African stool, Indian shawls, a "sprig muslin" tea set, and a handsome Canton

tea set brought back in the days when crockery was used as a ballast for the tea cargo.

★ ★ ★

Many and varied as the sources of information at the Society are, they still think they'd be stumped by a question the Historical Society of Pennsylvania was asked. "Do you have photographs of the expressions of the lions on statuary in Philadelphia?" was the eager inquiry.

They wonder when people will start asking about Boston's statuary and its expressions.

Profile of New England Historic Genealogical Society, featuring Librarian and *Register* Editor Arthur Adams. *Boston Sunday Globe*, January 17, 1954.

REVIEWS POST SERIAL

Melville C. Freeman of Kennebunkport, Me., author of "The Plymouth Adventure," which ran serially in the Boston Post, reviewed the historical novel at a meeting of the New England Historic Genealogical Society at their headquarters on Beacon Hill yesterday. Mrs. Charles H. Proctor of Swampscott, left, and Mrs. Henry Endicott of the Back Bay, welcomed Mr. Freeman.

An author event for Melville C. Freeman's *The Plymouth Adventure* at New England Historic Genealogical Society. NEHGS members Katherine (Sears) Endicott, Blanche (Walker) Pfaelzer, and Grace (Hopkins) Proctor poured tea after the event. *The Boston Post*, January 4, 1951.

From the Archives

New England Historic Genealogical Society photo and press release from 1947.

Makes Family Trees

ALTHOUGH NEW ENGLAND is supposed to be more ancestor-conscious than other parts of the country, the fact is that Dr. Arthur Adams, librarian at the New England Historic Genealogical Society, receives more requests for genealogical information from the West than he does from this corner of the country.

Dr. Adams is found at his desk on the third floor of the society's quarters at 9 Ashburton pl., every morning at 9, remains hard at work until 5, then strolls home to Pinckney st.

Dr. Adams, who will be 75 next May, is in "retirement." Five years ago, after 38 years as a professor at Trinity College in Hartford, he came to Boston to pursue full time what had been a lifelong part-time interest—genealogy and heraldry.

He is a man of many parts, a priest of the Protestant Episcopal Church, author of two books, Phi Beta Kappa (Rutgers), Fellow of the Royal Society of Literature, registrar general of the Society of Colonial Wars, and a member of countless clubs devoted to his hobbies and interests.

In addition to being librarian, he is also editor of the society's Register, a monthly publication.

Brief profile of much-admired Arthur Adams, New England Historic Genealogical Society Librarian and *Register* Editor. *Boston Post Magazine,* January 23, 1955.

The New England Historic Genealogical Society

requests the honor of your presence at the celebration of its

One Hundredth Anniversary

in Wilder Hall, 9 Ashburton Place, Boston

Saturday, March 17, 1945, at 11 o'clock

Address by Arthur Adams, Ph.D.

Professor of English, Trinity College

Buffet Luncheon at 12:30   Inspection of Building at 1:00

Admission card will be sent upon receipt of acceptance

Invitation to the New England Historic Genealogical Society's 100th anniversary celebration, 1945. Founder Charles Ewer was honored and a group of members visited the Old Granary Burying Ground on Tremont Street to view the new tombstone at Ewer's grave. William Prescott Greenlaw was also honored for fifty years as a staff member and officer. Greenlaw first joined New England Historic Genealogical Society as a researcher in 1891, progressed to librarian and assistant tresurer, and served on the council.

N. E. Historic Genealogical Society Observes 320th Anniversary of Mayflower Compact

OBSERVE 320th ANNIVERSARY OF MAYFLOWER COMPACT

Left to Right, Seated—William Greenlaw and Davenport Brown. Standing—James M. Hunnewell, Frederic A. Turner, Mrs. Joseph Curtis Howes and Rev. Dr. Phillips Endecott Osgood.

The 320th anniversary of the signing of the Mayflower Compact was celebrated with a special program by the New England Historic Genealogical Society at its headquarters, Wilder Hall, 9 Ashburton pl., yesterday afternoon.

Dr. Phillips Endecott Osgood, rector of Emmanuel Church, was the principal speaker. He reviewed the history of the compact and emphasized what it meant in the early days and today. He added that in these exciting days when nations are being overturned and countries in Europe are changing almost daily, a society such as the New England Historic Genealogical Society should make an extra effort to keep alive and active. Often in days of stress great organizations lost foothold and interest died out, but the observance of the Mayflower Compact should be kept up and societies which are keeping alive the history of both the country and the early families should be preserved, he declared.

Mrs. Joseph Curtis Howes of Brookline, curator of the society, read the compact. Frederic Alonzo Turner, vice president, presided in the absence of Pres. Frederick Silsbee Whitwell, who was unable to attend. Davenport Brown, chairman of the steering committee, was in charge of arrangements.

Anniversary of the signing of the Mayflower Compact at New England Historic Genealogical Society. *The Boston Daily Globe*, November 22, 1940.

New England Historic Genealogical Society

9 ASHBURTON PLACE, BOSTON, MASS.

Stated Meetings

WILDER HALL

AT 2.30 P. M.

October 6, 1937

"Tar and Feathers,"
By Frank Wilson Cheney Hersey, A. M.,
Instructor in English at Harvard University.

November 3

"Old Silver,"
By Amy Sacker,
Director of the School of Decorative Design,
Boston, Mass.
Illustrated with Examples.

December 1

"New England Architecture from the Puritan
to the Technocrat,"
By Ralph Adams Cram, Litt. D., LL. D.,
of Boston, Mass.
Under the auspices of the Women's Lecture Fund.

January 5, 1938

"Clipper Ships,"
By Rev. Charles Edwards Park, D. D.,
of Boston, Mass.
Illustrated with Lantern Slides.

February 2

ANNUAL MEETING
"Witchcraft,"
By George Lyman Kittredge, Litt. D., LL. D.,
of Cambridge, Mass.
Under the auspices of the George Lambert
Gould Lecture Fund.

March 2

"A True (?) Likeness of George Washington,"
By Frederick Foster, LL. B.,
of Brookline, Mass.
Illustrated with Lantern Slides.

April 6

"Massachusetts Under the Articles of
Confederation: Depression One Hundred
and Fifty Years Ago,"
By Robert Earle Moody, Ph. D.,
Professor of History, Boston University.
Under the auspices of the John Carroll Chase
Lecture Fund.

May 4

"The Face of the Land in Massachusetts,"
By Bradford Williams, Field Secretary,
The Trustees of Public Reservations.
Illustrated with Lantern Slides.

Architecture To Be Topic Of Lecture

Ralph Adams Cram To Talk Wednesday Afternoon

Mr. Ralph Adams Cram, the noted architect, will be the distinguished speaker at the last of this year's regular meetings of the New England Historic Genealogical Society next Wednesday afternoon at 2:30 in Wilder Hall. His lecture has a provocative title, "New England Architecture from the Puritan to the Technocrat."

After the lecture tea will be served. The hostesses for the afternoon will be Mrs. John Edward Kincaid, Mrs. Stanwood Gray Wellington, Mrs. Charles Collens, Mrs. Robert Cushman, Mrs. George C. Houser, Mrs. Otis Weld Richardson, Mrs. Francis G. Shaw, Jr., Mrs. Frederic Tudor, Miss Linda Collens and Miss Catharine Richardson.

TRANSCRIPT. SATURDAY, NOVEMBER 30, 1935

PERSONAL

Mrs. John C. Chase   (Dorothy Jarvie)

Who Will Be One of the Hostesses at the Meeting of the New England Historic Genealogical Society on Wednesday, Dec. 4, at Which Professor Samuel Eliot Morison Will Speak on the "Founding of Harvard College"

BOSTON TRAVELER, MONDAY, OCTOBER 17, 1938

'SILHOUETTES' SPEAKER

DORIS BURDICK

The Rev. Glenn Tilley Morse in his Newburyport pulpit as depicted by Miss Doris Burdick of Malden. Mr. Morse will speak on his hobby, "Silhouettes," tomorrow at 11 A. M. at 9 Ashburton place, starting a series of lectures on the history of arts and crafts, sponsored by the New England Historic Genealogical Society.

(*left*) Schedule of lectures at New England Historic Genealogical Society in 1937.

(*right*) Article lauding the upcoming lecture from legendary architect Ralph Adams Cram, December 1937.

(*left*) On December 4, 1935, Professor Samuel Eliot Morison gave an illustrated lecture on the founding of Harvard University at a New England Historic Genealogical Society meeting at Ashburton Place. A tea following the meeting was hosted by Florence Anne Chase, wife of John Carroll Chase, president of New England Historic Genealogical Society, 1922–1936. *Boston Evening Transcript*, November 30, 1935.

(*right*) The first lecture in a series on the history of arts and crafts in the Atkinson-Lancaster Room at New England Historic Genealogical Society. *Boston Traveler*, October 17, 1938.

N. E. Genealogical Society Prepares to Mark 90 Years of 'Family Tree' Work

Organization Started With Only Five Members— Now Has 2700

Preparing today for its 90th birthday, stronger by far than in the days of its youth, a venerable Boston institution in Ashburton place stands as an unperishing monument to the perennial interest in the family tree.

FAMOUS LIBRARY

The New England Historical and Genealogical Society, which will have been incorporated 90 years next March 18, began with five members. Today it has 2700 members, one of the finest libraries in the city and a roster of famous names, including the late King Albert of the Belgians, John Greenleaf Whittier, Thomas A. Edison, Alexander Graham Bell and former President Herbert Hoover, as well as hundreds of less famous persons, interested in their ancestry and the records of American families in the New England states.

Besides the library, where the public may now go to search its family records, the society has now the additional attraction of the treasured family relics of the Atkinson-Lancaster collection, housed in a specially constructed room and including many gorgeously carved pieces of furniture made in India and brought to Boston by early sea captains and other members of the families. The collection was left to the society, with a fund sufficient for its maintenance, by Dr. Lizzie Rose Daniel Atkinson.

The society was incorporated by a special act of the Legislature March

Library of the New England Historical and Genealogical Society in Ashburton place (above), and below, the society's museum showing the famous Atkinson-Lancaster collection of furniture and other objects, recently opened to the public.

18, 1845, and claims to be the first of its kind in the world. It owes its existence to the vision and foresight of five men, all of Boston: Charles Ewer, William Henry Montague, Lemuel Shattuck, John Wingate and Thornton and Samuel Gardner Blake.

24 ORIGINAL BOOKS

Starting with 24 bound books, 10 manuscripts and other odds and ends, the library now totals approximately 80,000 volumes. In 1898 it was voted to allow women to become members, and with a vanguard of 36 members they increased until two years ago nearly 50 per cent. of the membership was women.

The president of the society is John Carroll Chase of Derry, N. H., and its treasurer is James Melville Hunnewell of Boston. The curator of the museum is Mrs. Joseph Curtis Howes.

Mrs. Howes is a gracious, charming hostess.

Born in Somerville as Florence Reynolds Conant, her education was received in the public schools of that city where she prepared for college. She married in 1905 and was widowed in 1907. A special interest in her early days was "old English script." After the death of her husband she entered genealogical work. Her ancestry includes Pilgrim and Puritan stock, and her family tree includes John and Priscilla Alden, Roger Conant, the Rev. John Wilson, the Rev. Thomas Hooker and Edward Rawson.

BUILDING IMPOSING

Very imposing in its simple grandeur, the entrance to their building through the "Corridor of States" is beautified by the addition of stained glass windows and tablets in memory of those responsible for subscriptions and endowments. The library upstairs is most comfortably furnished, and daily numbers of people may be seen poring over old volumes. The officers of the society are glad to have the general public call. There are now more than 600 three-foot shelves filled with books and manuscripts which relate to every state in the union. Subject to proper limitations, books are loaned to those who cannot visit the library, and this service is one of the important functions of the institution and is one

---

OLD GOWNS AND BONNETS WORN AT MEETING OF N. E. HISTORIC GENEALOGICAL SOCIETY

Stanley D. Bean Lectures on Romance Associated With the Life of Whittier and the Merrimac Valley—Members of Reception Committee Wear Heirlooms

HOSTESSES AT MEETING OF HISTORIC GENEALOGICAL SOCIETY
Seated, Left to Right—Miss Elsie McCormack, Mrs Franklin E. Scotty, Miss Edith M. Tilley. Standing. Left to Right—Miss Margery Leavitt, Mrs George C. Houser, Mrs Theodore L. Smith, Mrs Walter M. Bush, Mrs Ralph C. Estes, Miss Elizabeth Fowle, Mrs John Carroll Chase.

Romance in the story of the Merrimac Valley, associated with the life of John G. Whittier, the Quaker poet, as told yesterday afternoon by Stanley Oscar Bean of Amesbury at the meeting of the New England Historic Genealogical Society, was accentuated by picturesque gowns and millinery of from 60 to 80 years ago worn by the 11 members of the reception committee.

Some of the relics were heirlooms from Concord. That worn by Mrs Augustus Hemenway Eustis of Milton was a reproduction of one originally worn by a member of Louisa M. Alcott's family.

The others were worn by Mrs John Carroll Chase, Mrs Ralph C. Estes, Mrs George C. Houser, Mrs Franklin E. Scotty, Mrs Theodore L. Smith, Mrs Alden A. Thorndike and Misses Elizabeth Fowle, Magery A. Leavitt, Elsie McCormack and Edith M. Tilley.

The monthly report of the society's secretary, Henry Edwards Scott, showed six deaths among the members, 14 new ones admitted, and gifts of genealogies of the Closson and Hamilton families.

John Carroll Chase presided.

A lecture at New England Historic Genealogical Society was complemented by notable gowns worn by members of the reception committee, including a reproduction of a gown worn by Louisa May Alcott's relative, 1933.

Profile of New England Historic Genealogical Society, highlighting the recent Atkinson-Lancaster bequest which had belonged to Lizzie Daniel Rose Atkinson, M.D. This was the most significant gift of the 1920s and 30s for the organization. *Boston Traveler*, December 19, 1934.

LIVING TABLEAUX IN GENEALOGICAL HALL

Historic Characters Step Out of Frames and Talk

Mrs Frost, Mrs Converse and Mrs Peirce Relate Noted Lives

Three portraiture monologues illustrative of Massachusetts history constituted the Wednesday afternoon patriotic entertainment of the New England Historic Genealogical Society in its auditorium, 9 Ashburton pl, yesterday.

The entertainment was a trio of living tableaux reproducing well-known portraits of historical personages.

On the raising of a curtain the living subject was revealed on the stage, enclosed within a gilt frame. "Coming to life," each subject in turn told his or her romantic life story, made certain observations on the changes in local manners and customs since they were actually on earth, then retired into the frame and reassumed the stolidity and dumbness of paint and canvas again.

Mrs Verda Frost, made up in imitation of a portrait of Rebecca Rawson in the Genealogical Society's building, told with rare feeling the tragic story of the daughter of Edward Rawson, Puritan Secretary of the Commonwealth, whose estate 250 years ago extended along the north side of Bromfield st, from Washington st to Province st.

Mrs Cyrus H. Converse gave a very creditable reproduction of a portrait in the Essex Institute, Salem, of Sir William Pepperell, conqueror of Louisburg, C B, and one of the earliest New Englanders knighted, incidentally reviewing outstanding details of his career.

Mrs George L. Peirce, as a living copy of a portrait of Sally Barrett Cabot of about the Revolutionary period, related an amusing budget of family gossip of her period.

Mrs Howard H. C. Bingham had the role of a librarian actually figuring as announcer of the changes. Miss Grace Cummings and Mrs F. A. Flanders were pages.

Appropriate incidental music was furnished by Miss Barbara Whitney on the harp.

The three monologues were prepared by Mrs Isabel Cushman Nason from authentic family data in the Genealogical Society's library, or that of the Massachusetts Historical Society.

New England Historic Genealogical Society

9 ASHBURTON PLACE, BOSTON

A Stated Meeting of the Society will be held in Wilder Hall,

WEDNESDAY, DECEMBER 6, 1933,
At 2.30 P.M.

LEONARD CRASKE,
of Boston,

will present

"Miracles in Color,"

Illustrated with Photographs in Color.

Provided by an Anonymous Lecture Fund.

Mr. Craske, who is best known in New England as the sculptor of the "American Doughboy" memorial at Amesbury and the "Gloucester Fisherman" overlooking Gloucester Harbor, has made an intensive study of present-day color photography, with results surpassing any hitherto attained in this art. Most of his experiments have been made in or near Gloucester, whither he will take his audience in the lecture.

Hostesses

Mrs. Charles Gaston Smith

Mrs. William Alexander Gaston	Mrs. Willis Stratton Shepard
Mrs. Percival Hall Lombard	Mrs. Phineas Warren Sprague
Mrs. George Megrew	Mrs. Alden Augustus Thorndike
Mrs. F. Wainwright Perkins	Mrs. Stanwood Gray Wellington

Mrs. Richard Wheatland

Those wishing to avoid the stairway may reach the auditorium floor through a short foot-passage from Allston Street at the rear of the new building of the Metropolitan District Commission.

This announcement, when endorsed by a member, will admit guests. Members may obtain at the office of the Recording Secretary a limited number of additional copies of this notice, until the supply is exhausted.

Henry Edwards Scott,
Recording Secretary.

No admittance after 2.45 P. M.

(*left*) Newspaper article detailing the April 1930 performance of *Portraiture Monologues*, written by Isabelle (Cushman) Nason, a member of New England Historic Genealogical Society.

(*right*) Announcement of lecture by sculptor Leonard Craske at New England Historic Genealogical Society, 1933. Craske is known for the Fisherman's Memorial in Gloucester, Massachusetts.

Scenes from 9 Ashburton Place

Sixth location of New England Historic Genealogical Society, 1912 to 1964.

Conversation Room.

The John Foster Memorial Council Room.

Marshall P. Wilder Hall, 1914.

9 Ashburton Place (second from the right) before occupancy of New England Historic Genealogical Society.

Façade of 9 Ashburton Place.

Meeting Hall, 1913.

The Robert Henry Eddy Memorial Rooms with *Register* Editor Henry Edwards Scott in the background and staff member Mabel Chapin in the foreground, 1913.

Construction of 99–101 Newbury Street in 1928 as a three-story building for the New England Trust Company. New England Historic Genealogical Society moved into this location in 1964.

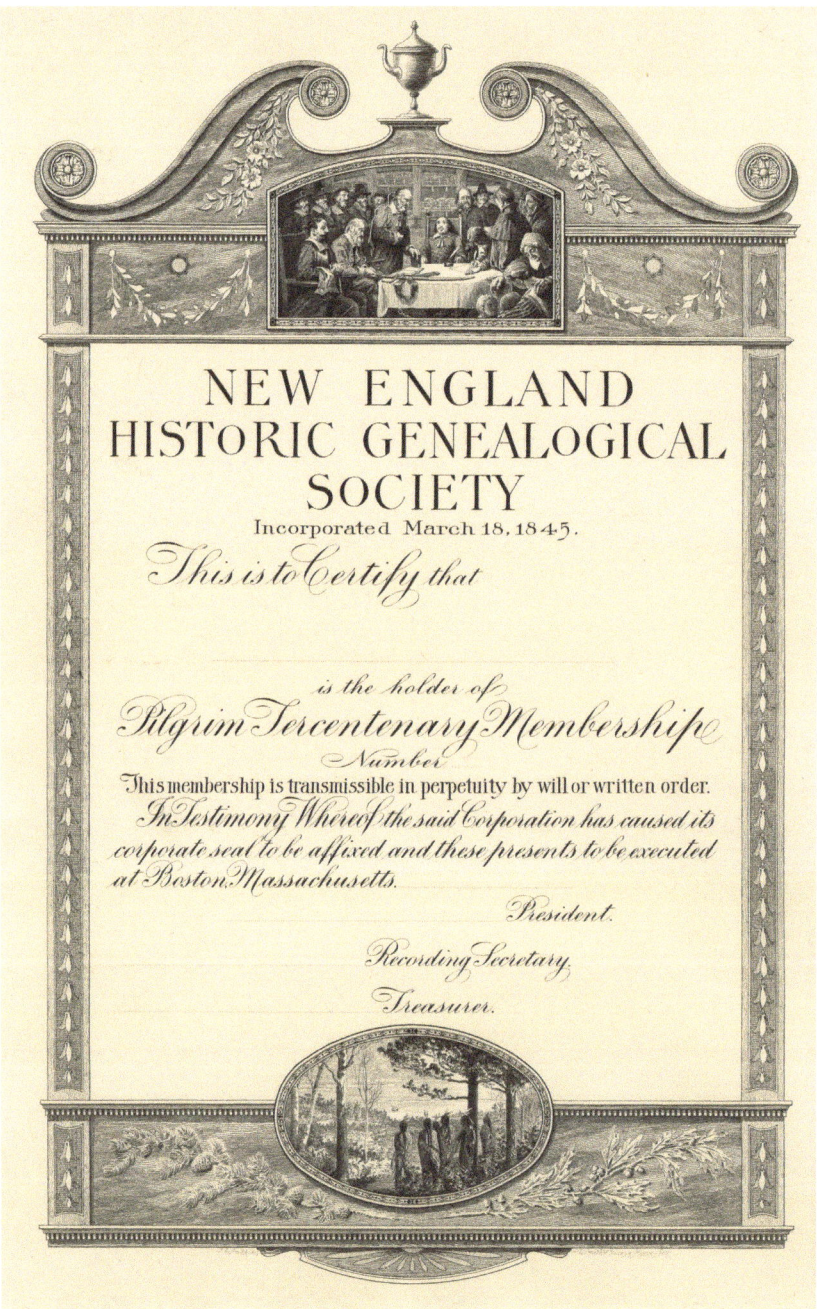

In 1918, New England Historic Genealogical Society created the Pilgrim Tercentenary Membership in celebration of the 300th anniversary of the Pilgrims' landing at Plymouth, Massachusetts. This membership was available from February 5, 1919, to January 1, 1921, and cost $300.

Scenes from 18 Somerset Street

Fifth location of New England Historic Genealogical Society, 1871 to 1912.

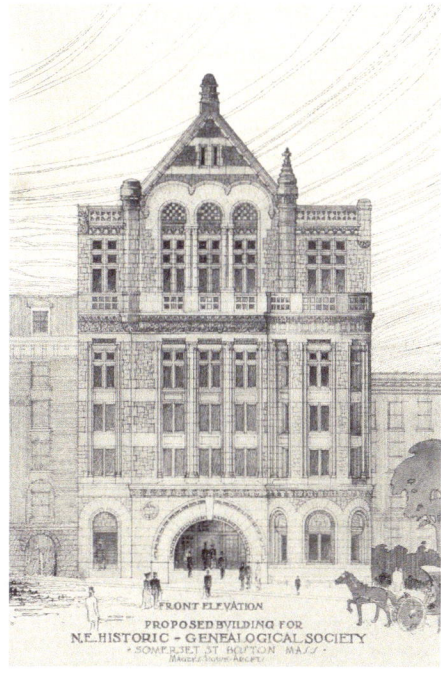

Artist's rendering of design for New England Historic Genealogical Society headquarters at Somerset Street that was not used.

Reading Room, 1895.

Another view of the Reading Room.

Four Homes

13 (later numbered 17) Bromfield Street, Boston. The third floor of the building next to the 19 Ford awning was the fourth home of New England Historic Genealogical Society, 1858 to 1871.

5 Tremont Street, Boston. A room on the third floor was the third home of New England Historic Genealogical Society, 1851 to 1858.

City Building, Court Square, Boston. Room 9 on the third floor of the hip-roofed building on the right was the first home of New England Historic Genealogical Society, February 1846 to October 1847. A room on the ground floor of the center building (then called Massachusetts Black, later the Sherman House) was the second home, 1847 to 1851.

Firsts

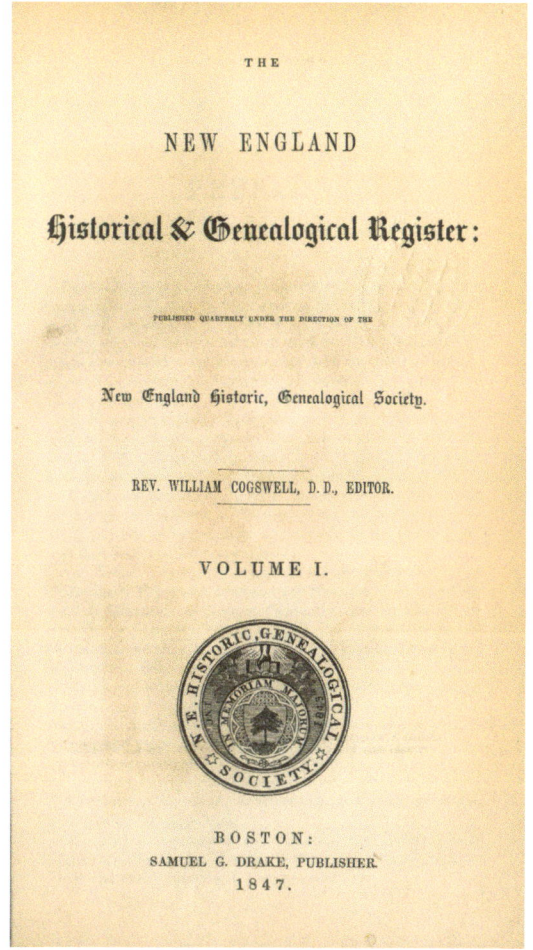

First published in 1847, the *New England Historical and Genealogical Register* was established as a quarterly journal to rescue neglected public records; serve members in furthering research, discussion, and writing about New England's puritan fathers; and fill the void left by historical literature in supplying information on families.

Samuel G. Drake, one of the founders of New England Historic Genealogical Society, insisted that a unified structure must be followed when publishing genealogical data. By 1870, *Register* style was presented as the standard for genealogical writing.

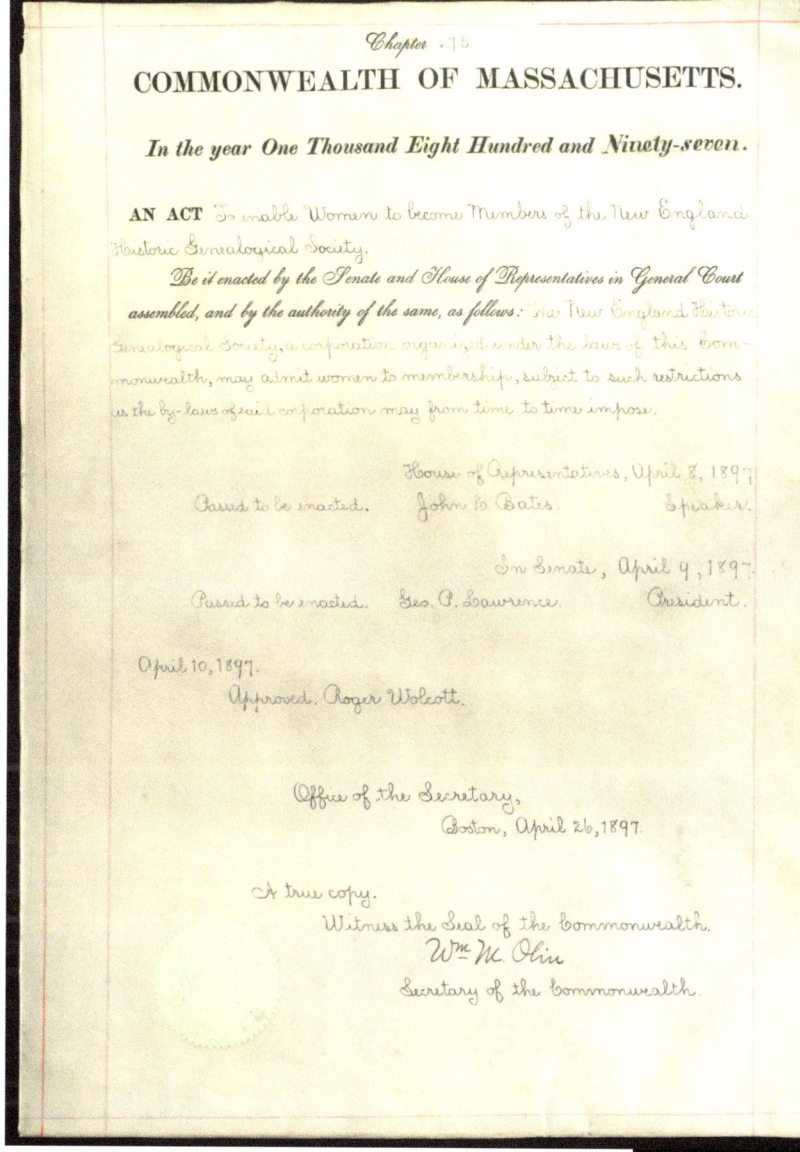

New England Historic Genealogical Society members voted to admit women in January 1897. After approval from the Massachusetts legislature and the governor, the bylaws were updated to reflect the change.

Family Treasures

Lemuel Shattuck (1793–1859), one of the founders and the first vice president of New England Historic Genealogical Society, commissioned Bass Otis (1784–1861) to paint this family portrait in 1850. From left to right are Shattuck; daughters Rebecca Elizabeth (1829–51), Frances Minot (1835–50), Sarah White (1827–63, in foreground), Clarissa Baxter (1831–58), and Miriam Stedman (1833–1909); and Shattuck's wife, Clarissa Baxter (1797–1871).

John Albion Andrew (1818–67) was the twenty-fifth Governor of Massachusetts. Andrew was elected president of New England Historic Genealogical Society in 1866. In his one inaugural address, he enthusiastically and forcefully stressed the importance and relevance of genealogy, biography, and history. This miniature is Thomas Ridgeway Gould's circa 1875 study for the grave statue of the governor that now stands on Andrew's tomb in the Old Ship Burying Ground in Hingham, Massachusetts.

OCTOBER, 1858.

CHARLES EWER, *President.*
LEMUEL SHATTUCK, *Vice President.*
SAMUEL G. DRAKE, *Pres., Cor. Sec. and Editor.*
WILLIAM H. MONTAGUE, *Treasurer.*
E. B. DEARBORN, *Librarian.*
SAMUEL H. RIDDEL, *Cor. and Rec. Sec.*

WILLIAM COGSWELL, *Editor.*
DAVID PULSIFER, *Rec. Sec. and Librarian.*
JOSEPH B. FELT, *President and Editor.*
LUCIUS R. PAIGE, *Vice President.*
NATHANIEL B. SHURTLEFF, *V. P., Cor. Sec. and Editor.*
THOMAS B. WYMAN, JR., *Librarian.*

CHARLES MAYO, *Recording Secretary.*
FREDERIC KIDDER, *Treasurer.*
WILLIAM B. TRASK, *Editor and Librarian.*
TIMOTHY FARRAR, *Vice Pres. and Editor.*
WILLIAM WHITING, *President.*
LUTHER FARNHAM, *Librarian.*

JOHN WARD DEAN,
FRANCIS BRINLEY, *Historiographer.*
JOSEPH PALMER, *Historiographer.*
ISAAC CHILD, *Treasurer.*
WILLIAM M. CORNELL, *Recording Secretary.*
EDWARD HOLDEN, *Librarian.*

In October 1858, New England Historic Genealogical Society compiled this photo montage of twenty-four of its earliest officers, the oldest group image we have of the organization's leadership and a sign of its growth.

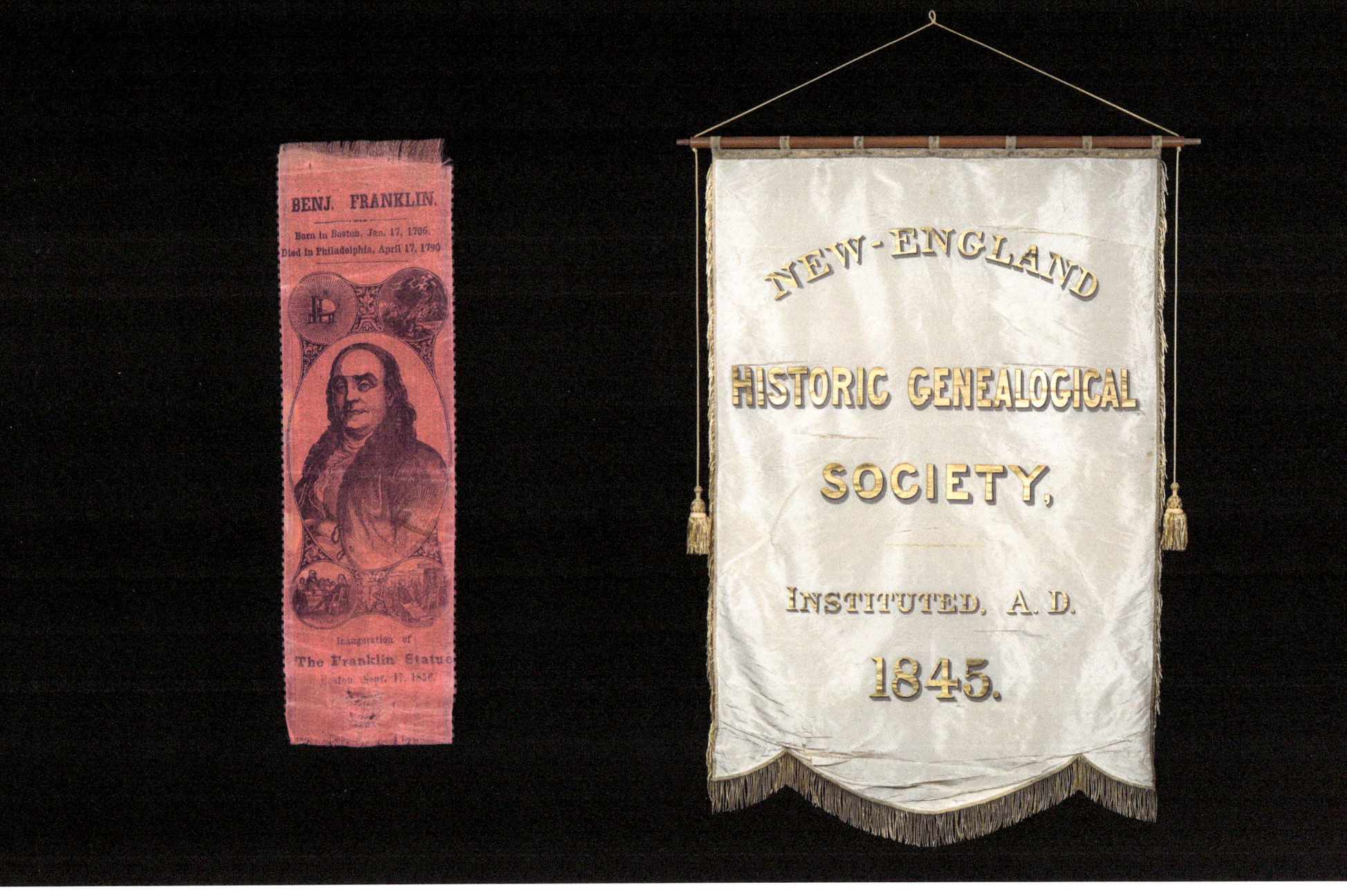

In September 1856, New England Historic Genealogical Society participated in the unveiling of a sculpture of Benjamin Franklin by Richard Saltonstall Greenough in front of the former Boston City Hall. To commemorate the event, Boston printer George C. Jenks was hired to make red silk ribbons featuring a portrait of Franklin by Boston engraver Samuel E. Brown. Greenough's life-size statue of Franklin is now an important stop on the Freedom Trail at Boston's Old City Hall.

New England Historic Genealogical Society members likely held this banner at the unveiling of Greenough's sculpture of Franklin in 1856. The festivities were described in the October 11, 1856 issue of *Ballou's Pictorial Drawing-Room Companion* as "a display, in point of numbers and character, far surpassing the most brilliant parades that ever graced any previous occasion."

This first piece of furniture in the possession of New England Historic Genealogical Society once belonged to the Rev. John Pierpont (1785–1866), minister of Hollis Street Church in Boston from 1839 until 1845. The revolving mahogany table was made in England circa 1825–1835 by an unknown craftsman. Samuel G. Drake (1798–1875), one of the founding members, is said to have purchased this desk at auction just about a year after the organization was incorporated.

The table in its current location at the headquarters of New England Historic Genealogical Society at 99–101 Newbury Street, outside the Board Room on the third floor.

The Pierpont table in the rented room on the third floor of the City Building on Court Square in downtown Boston, the first location of New England Historic Genealogical Society, ca. 1847–1851.

Our Founding

Samuel G. Drake Esqr Corresponding Secretary of the
New England Historic Genealogical Society. Boston
                                    Quincy 1. August 1845
Sir

            I have received your Letter of 6 Feb'y last
communicating to me the honour done me by the New-England
Historic Genealogical Society, by electing me an honorary member of
that Institution. I accept gratefully this testimonial of esteem, and
shall be happy if it may be in my power to contribute in any manner to
the laudable purposes of the Society
            I am with great respect, Sir
                your humble and obed't Serv't
                        J. Q. Adams

John Quincy Adams was elected to be a member of New
England Historic Genealogical Society on February 20, 1845,
just before our incorporation.

Charles Ewer was the first president of New England Historic Genealogical Society.
He served six terms as president.

Chap. 152.

COMMONWEALTH OF MASSACHUSETTS.

In the year One Thousand Eight Hundred and Forty-five.

AN ACT to incorporate the New-England Historic-Genealogical Society.

Be it enacted by the Senate and House of Representatives in General Court assembled, and by the authority of the same, as follows: Charles Ewer, J. Wingate Thornton, Joseph Willard, their associates and successors, are hereby made a corporation by the name of the New-England Historic-Genealogical Society for the purpose of collecting, preserving and occasionally publishing genealogical and historical matter relating to early New-England families, and for the establishment and maintenance of a cabinet, and for these purposes shall have all the powers and privileges and be subject to all the duties, requirements and liabilities set forth in the forty-fourth chapter of the Revised Statutes. Section 2. The said corporation may hold and possess real and personal estate to an amount not exceeding twenty thousand dollars.

House of Representatives,   March 17, 1845.
Passed to be enacted.   Tim H. Watley Jun., Speaker.

In Senate,   March 18, 1845.
Passed to be enacted.   Levi Lincoln,   President.

March 18, 1845.
Approved.
Geo. N. Briggs.

Secretary's Department, Boston, March 29, A.D. 1869.
I certify that the foregoing is a true copy.
Witness the Seal of the Commonwealth.
[signature]
Secretary of the Commonwealth.

New England Historic Genealogical Society was established by a group of five Bostonians: Charles Ewer (1790–1853), Lemuel Shattuck (1793–1859), Samuel Gardner Drake (1798–1875), John Wingate Thornton (1818–1878), and William Henry Montague (1804–1889). These articles of incorporation from March 18, 1845, state our then humble purpose as "collecting, preserving and occasionally publishing, genealogical and historical matter, relating to early New-England families . . ."

Board and Council

Staff

Administration

D. Brenton Simons
President and CEO

Ryan J. Woods
Executive Vice President and Chief Operating Officer

Susan B. Fugliese
Vice President for Advancement

Beth A. Brown
Assistant Vice President for Advancement

Business Development and Sales

Don Reagan
Director of Business Development

Henry Hornblower
Marketing Manager

Rick Park
Sales Coordinator

Creative Services and Website Development

Claire Vail
Director of Creative and Digital Strategy

Jim Power
Communications Manager

Amy Joyce
Digital/Print Graphic Designer

Don LeClair
Associate Director Database and Search Systems

Thomas Grebenchick
Web Content Coordinator

Rachel Adams
Database Services Volunteer Coordinator

Andy Hanson-Dvoracek
Systems Architect

Creative Services and Website Development, cont.

Molly Rogers
Digital Database Coordinator

Samuel Paine Sturgis III
Digital Collections Administrator

Alicia Crane Williams
Genealogist

Development

Ted MacMahon
Senior Gift Planning Officer

Stacie Madden
Director of Development

Steven L. Solomon
Senior Philanthropy Officer

Kaitlin Hurley
Development and Stewardship Coordinator

Education and Programs

Ginevra Morse
Director of Education and Online Programs

Tricia Labbe
Education Coordinator

Dustin Axe
Youth Genealogy Curriculum Coordinator

Facilities

Matt Ottinger
Director of Facilities

John Phlo
Digitization Assistant and Facilities Coordinator

Michael McIntyre
Building and Maintenance Assistant

Finance

Bruce Bernier
Chief Financial Officer

Michael Forbes
Senior Accountant

Megan Peterson
Accountant

Emma Brightbill
Accounts Receivable Associate

Melane Barrios
Accounts Payable Associate

Fine Art

Curt DiCamillo
Curator of Special Collections

Heritage Tours

Cy Britt
Director of Heritage Tours

Human Resources

Michelle Major
Director of Human Resources

Information Technology

Steven Shilcusky
Director of Information Technology

Wes Matthews
Database Manager

Library

Jean Maguire
Library Director

David Allen Lambert
Chief Genealogist

Rhonda R. McClure
Senior Genealogist

Tom Dreyer
Genealogist

Alice Kane
*Library Patron Services and
Consultations Manager*

Melanie McComb
Genealogist

Tricia Healy Mitchell
Genealogist

Ann Lawthers
Genealogist

Library, cont.

Cheryl Gilmore-Thys
*Consultation and Copy
Services Coordinator*

Helen Herzer
Volunteer Coordinator

Library Collection Services

Timothy G. X. Salls
*Manager of Manuscript
Collections*

Anne Meringolo
*Library Collection
Services Manager*

Olga Tugarina
*Library Collection
Services Assistant*

Todd Pattison
Conservator

Sally Benny
Curator of Digital Collections

Library Collection Services, cont.

Judith M. Lucey
Senior Archivist

Gaia Cloutier
Project Archivist

Member Services

Kathleen Mackenzie
Manager of Member Services

Kyle Lindsay
Member Services Associate

Valerie Beaudrault
Visitor Services Representative

Maria Kuntz
Visitor Services Representative

Shannon Lavoie
Member Services Associate

Signature and Literary Events

Margaret M. Talcott
Director of Signature and Literary Events

Courtney Reardon
Events Coordinator

The Wyner Family Jewish Heritage Center

Rachel King
Director

Stephanie Call
Associate Director of Archives and Education

Kelsey Sawyer
Reference and Photo Archivist

Lindsay Murphy
Collections Archivist

Brittany Contratto
Digital Projects Archivist

Publications

Sharon Inglis
Publishing Director

Scott C. Steward
Editor-in-Chief

Cécile Engeln
Assistant Publishing Director

Lynn Betlock
Managing Editor, American Ancestors

Christopher C. Child
Senior Genealogist of the Newbury Street Press

Kyle Hurst
Senior Genealogist of the Newbury Street Press

Meaghan E. H. Siekman
Genealogist of the Newbury Street Press

Henry B. Hoff, CG, FASG
Editor of the Register

Publications, cont.

Ellen Maxwell
Publications Design Manager

Jean Powers
Senior Editor

Carolyn Sheppard Oakley
Editor and Creative Director

Eileen Pironti
Genealogist of the Newbury Street Press

Susan Donnelly
Genealogist of the Newbury Street Press

Research Services

Lindsay Fulton
Director of Research Services

Sarah Dery
Research Services Manager

Sheilagh Doerfler
Senior Researcher

Katrina Fahy
Senior Researcher

James Heffernan
Senior Researcher

Danielle Cournoyer
Researcher

Michelle Doherty
Researcher

Research Services, cont.

Geneva Cann
Researcher

Zachary Garceau
Researcher

Pam Guye Holland
Researcher

Andrew Krea
Researcher

Raymond Addison
Researcher

Maureen Carey
Researcher

Jennica Bayne
Researcher

Research Services, cont.

Chloe Jones
Researcher

Hallie Borstel
Researcher

Jen Shakshober
Researcher

Elizabeth Peay
Researcher

Erin Connelly
Researcher

Photo Credits

Cover: **front**: (t, l) NEHGS, (t, m and t, r) Claire Vail, (b, l and b, m) NEHGS; **back**: (t, l) NEHGS, (m) Claire Vail, (t, r) NEHGS, (b, l) Claire Vail, (b, r) NEHGS.

Introduction: **ix**: NEHGS.

2000 to 2020: **x**: NEHGS; **1–3**: NEHGS; **4**: Pierce Harman Photography; **5**: (t, l and b, l) Pierce Harman Photography, (r) NEHGS; **6**: Pierce Harman Photography; **7**: (t, l) Roger Farrington, (t, r) Pierce Harman Photography, (b, l) Roger Farrington, (b, r) Roger Farrington; **8**: Roger Farrington; **9**: (l, and t, r and m, r) Pierce Harman Photography, (b, r) Xingyan Xu; **10–12**: NEHGS; **13**: (t and l) Claire Vail, (b) NEHGS; **14**: (l and b) Jean Powers, (t, r) NEHGS; **15**: (t, l) Pierce Harman Photography, (b and r) Jean Powers; **16**: NEHGS; **17**: (t) Pierce Harman Photography, (l and b) NEHGS; **18, 19**: NEHGS; **20**: (t and b) NEHGS, (m and r) Claire Vail; **21**: (t, l) courtesy of *Finding Your Roots with Henry Louis Gates, Jr.*, (b, l and t, r and b, r) NEHGS; **22, 23**: NEHGS; **24**: (b, l) Scott Steward, (t and m and r) NEHGS; **25**: (t) NEHGS, (b) Claire Vail; **26–28**: NEHGS; **29**: (l and t, r) NEHGS, (b, r) Claire Vail; **30–31**: NEHGS.

1950 to 2000: **32**: NEHGS; **33**: (t and l): NEHGS, (r) Martha Holmes; **34–44**: NEHGS; **45**: (l) from The Boston Globe. © 1954 Boston Globe Media Partners. All rights reserved. Used under license, (r) "Chronological Events of the Society 7 January 1931 to 2 February 1955," Proceedings (Newspaper) 1931–1935, NEHGS Institutional Archives.

1900 to 1950: **46**: NEHGS; **47**: "Chronological Events of the Society 7 January 1931 to 2 February 1955," Proceedings (Newspaper) 1931–1935, NEHGS Institutional Archives; **48**: from The Boston Globe. © 1940 Boston Globe Media Partners. All rights reserved. Used under license; **49**: "Chronological Events of the Society 7 January 1931 to 2 February 1955," Proceedings (Newspaper) 1931–1935, NEHGS Institutional Archives; **50**: "Chronological Events of the Society 7 January 1931 to 2 February 1955," Proceedings (Newspaper) 1931–1935, NEHGS Institutional Archives; **51**: "Chronological Events of the Society 7 January 1931 to 2 February 1955," Proceedings (Newspaper) 1931–1935, NEHGS Institutional Archives; **52–55**: NEHGS.

1845 to 1900: **56–57**: NEHGS; **58–60**: Gavin Ashworth; **61**: (l) NEHGS, (r) Gavin Ashworth; **62–63**: NEHGS.